The Andragogic Learning Center

A Field Study in Social Work Education

Moshe Sonnheim
and
Shlomit Lehman

UNIVERSITY PRESS OF AMERICA,® INC.

Lanham • Boulder • New York • Toronto • Plymouth, UK

Copyright © 2010 by
University Press of America,® Inc.
4501 Forbes Boulevard
Suite 200
Lanham, Maryland 20706
UPA Acquisitions Department (301) 459-3366

Estover Road
Plymouth PL6 7PY
United Kingdom

Library of Congress Control Number: 2009936137
ISBN: 978-0-7618-4947-6 (paperback : alk. paper)
eISBN: 978-0-7618-4948-3

∞ ™ The paper used in this publication meets the minimum requirements of American
National Standard for Information Sciences—Permanence of Paper for Printed
Library Materials, ANSI Z39.48-1992.

Contents

Illustrations

Tables

Figures

Acknowledgments

This Monograph is supported by a Grant from Bar Ilan University, and is a culmination of my:

Fifty years as social worker, supervisor, and teacher.
Twenty-four of those years working in Givat Shmuel. A small town in Israel.
And eight of those years directing and researching an Andragogic Learning
    Center in that town.

Thus, my thanks are due to more people than I can enumerate individually in these short pages.

I have, therefore, chosen those who stand out in my memory.

My teachers at the University of Pennsylvania School of Social Work, especially Professor Helen U. Phillips; and at the School of Applied Social Sciences, Case Western Reserve University, especially Professors John Turner and George Levinger, who taught me, respectively, feeling, doing, and thinking.

My colleagues at the Bar Ilan University School of Social Work. Professors Ben Lappin and Frank Loewenberg, Dr. Aharon York, and, especially, Professor Reuven Schindler, who approved and supported the Project throughout those exciting years. Reuven Miller, Director of Field Work. And, of course, my research and teaching partner, Dr. Shlomit Auman Lehman!

Yaacov "Yankele" Vismonski, Head (Mayor) of the Local Council, Givat Shmuel, who believed in the mutual benefit of such a Project to the University, the town, and its citizens.

Haim Cohen, Director of Social Welfare Services, Givat Shmuel, who gave freely of his time as Supervisor, Liaison, and Full partner in our Project.

Efrat Lavie and Hannah Greenfeld, Senior Social Workers, and Supervisors, who made us feel a part of the network of social services.

The good people of Givat Shmuel, who literally adopted us and taught us how functional "dysfunctional" families can be.

Tamar Gazit Cohen and Anat Bart who served as "judges" of rankings.

Orly Levanon and Benny Maoz, who "excelled" the raw data of over 700 Questionnaires.

Amitai Abramovitch, our statistician and sounding board, who crafted the dry figures into understandable Tables and Graphs.

Janice Weinstein, who bravely mastered my handwriting and transcribed it into the pages you are about to read.

Benjie Herskowitz, who patiently and professionally prepared our manuscript for typesetting.

And, finally, but no less important, my wife, Jolene, and daughters Ada and Idit, who often were asleep when I returned at midnight to our home in Jerusalem from Givat Shmuel (an hour and a half ride away).

And Bingo, our faithful dog (now deceased), who greeted me with bark and lick, whatever the hour!

Introduction

This Monograph examines an eight-year Field Study in Social Work Education at the Bar Ilan University School of Social Work in Israel. We will present the philosophy underlying the Study, the process of "selling" the idea to the partners in the Study, the key elements in the Study, literature surveys before and after the Study, design and methodology of the Study, analysis of results, and implications for Social Work education. A separate section will include personal observations by Study participants-Faculty, Agency, Community, and Students.

Chapter One

The Andragogic Learning Center:
A Field Study in
Social Work Education

A HISTORY OF THE FIELD STUDY

The Bar Ilan School of Social Work, established in 1966, served at the time of the study, more than 700 students on campus (at present, 24,500 students), including 15 doctoral candidates and over 200 Masters degree students. The B.S.W. Program, since its inception, has emphasized Social Group Work. Therefore, second-year students must choose between two Sequences-Group Work/Case Work or Group Work/Community Organization. The faculty of the latter Sequence generally limited its numbers to fifteen to twenty students. The Field Study introduced a third, experimental sequence, "Multi-Method" (for want of a better title), beginning in 1990. This Sequence, too, was limited to a small group of students (10–12, according to the terms of the Study Grant).

Our story began, however, in 1974, when the Senior author was hired as a full-time Lecturer at the School of Social Work. With long experience as worker and supervisor in the field in the United States and Israel, and with an M.S.W. in Social Group Work and a D.S.W. in Community Organization, and Case Work in Mental Health, he received an interesting and challenging teaching load. This included courses in First-year Basics in Social Work, Second-year Methods courses in Casework, Group Work, and Community Organization for Group Work students, and Supervision of a Field Unit of eight Second-year students in the neighboring community of Givat Shmuel.

Thus began the Senior author's twenty-four year association with that small community of approximately 10,000 people (13,000 at the time of the study). Thus began the development of the idea of a Multi-Method Learning Center which we hoped would differ considerably from existing models of Learning Centers in the United States and Israel.

Underlying Philosophy

A recurring theme in Social Work education literature (at the time of our Proposal) was that Field Education is an integral part of the total curriculum of professional education (Kindelsperger, 1968; Schubert, 1969). Goldstein (1984) even provided a problem-solving paradigm consistent with an integrative approach. In 1993, however, he noted integration is difficult to attain. He even suggested shifting the "emphasis of education for practice from the class to the field." (Goldstein, 1993. 165–182) (especially 166, 168). In 2001, he focused on experiential learning as "a means of complementing and integrating class and field (Goldstein, 2001).Hamilton and Else (1983) discussed the principles shaping field education, and dealt with the principles of integration and transferability. All the authors, however, tended to maintain the traditional dichotomy between class and field instruction, while Schneck (1995) viewed the field teacher "as one who bridges the theoretical with the actual."

We proposed uniting class and field instruction in the person of one faculty instructor in a learning "module" (Learning Center) designed to maximize integration and transferability of values, knowledge, and interventive techniques ("skill") among Methods and among agencies. This faculty member (the Senior author) would teach all three Methods courses to the same small group of 10–12 students selected from those interested in volunteering for the Learning Center. He would also supervise half the Unit, while the Director of the local Welfare Office would supervise the other half.

The workload of each student would include 3 cases, 2 groups, and a community project (with a variety of age groups and problems). Thus, core concepts of intervention relevant to all three Methods, as well as Method-unique concepts, could be applied in practice. Students could allocate their fourteen hours of field work flexibly (i.e., in relation to client need rather than in relation to a required "two field days").

Class and field instruction would be given in the community itself. That is, the students would work in various settings (Family and Community Services, Schools, Community Centers), but their "home base" would be in a separate structure which would serve as the Learning Center. In practice, only the Community Organization course was taught in the "home base" (a bureaucratic accomplishment in itself), and all the supervision, consistent with the philosophy that students and faculty should spend as much time as possible in the community served.

The contractual partner for the Field Study would be the Local Council, and the local Welfare Office would be the vehicle for student assignments. This framework was based on our belief that a School of Social Work must share the educational process with the community which it serves, and not simply with the individual agencies within it. Moreover, we felt that the University itself should be the third partner in that process. Toward that end, we planned (and executed) Colloquia which involved other University Departments (such as Political Science), and which were held alternately in the University and Givat Shmuel.

Expanding our cooperative philosophy, we suggested (and established) a Steering Committee consisting of the Chairman of the Local Council (equivalent to a Mayor), the Dean of the School of Social Work and his Administrative Assistant, the Director of the local Welfare Office, the Coordinator of Field Work and his Secretary, a community representative, a student representative, and the Senior author (who would be responsible to the Committee as well as to the Dean).

Although there were descriptions of structure and location of field placements (see Hamilton and Else, 1983, 23–32), we found a paucity of research on Learning Centers since their establishment in the 1960's (Caroff & Mailick, 1980; Elad, 1989). Therefore, we recommended a research component in the Study Proposal, and added the Research Coordinator to the Steering Committee.

"Selling" the Idea

Selling the idea was a two-year community planning process which was an experience in itself. I (the Senior author) spent untold hours with the various potential partners to the Field Education Study.

The Director of the local Social Services (Welfare) Office was a Doctoral student at the School of Social Work, and had several years of an excellent working relationship with me (I had been his Master's Thesis Advisor). In addition, he had an excellent relationship with the Chairman of the Local Council and with a relatively stable, core staff of local civil service employees (e.g., Director of Educational Services, Director of Youth Services) who were interested in a high level of professional services.

The Chairman of the Local Council was extremely interested in strong ties with the University because of the personal and community prestige such an association would bring, and, I think, because of a genuine interest in serving his constituents.

The Dean of the School of Social Work embraced the idea with open arms because, as a teacher of Social Policy, he also believed in community involvement on the part of the University. He and his Administrative Assistant invested much time in meetings with the Chairman of the Local Council, the Director of the Social Services Office, and the University Administration (particularly, the Budget Director).

Fellow faculty members, in spite of some early reservations, were quite supportive. The fact that I was the only faculty member with experience in all three Social Work Methods, that I had a reputation as an excellent teacher and supervisor, and that I knew the community of Givat Shmuel, made it easier to deal with their questions.

1. Could such a small community provide 36 cases, 24 groups, and 12 community projects per year? In practice, the cases were provided, there were sometimes less groups, and several students worked with the same project.
2. Would second- and/or third-year students participate in the Learning Center? This question was related to the question of whether second-year students from the Group Work/Casework Sequence could switch to the third-year Group Work/Community Organization Sequence after "tasting" Community Organization in the Learning Center? For a variety of reasons, which we will discuss later, only second-year students comprised the Learning Center Sequence, and they were not permitted to switch to Group Work/Community Organization in their third and final year.
3. Would students be willing and disciplined enough to attend a University course (Community Organization) outside the "ivory tower," and would the University approve such a move? In both cases, the answer was "Yes!" A bit apprehensively, however, the University required a carefully-worded logo-"The Local Council Givat Shmuel: Learning Project in Cooperation with Bar Ilan University School of Social Work."
4. Why should the Learning Center be located in Givat Shmuel? In addition to reasons stated above, I emphasized:
    a. Its proximity to the University (allowing students to return to other campus courses after their Community Organization course; allowing flexibility in allocating their fourteen hours of Field Work).
    b. Its small geographic area (making it an "encompassible" community by foot and by feeling).
    c. Its relatively small, stable population which was becoming more heterogeneous culturally and socioeconomically.
    d. Its high degree of inter-organizational cooperation
    e. Its rich range of professional services in proportion to its population.
    f. A relationship between the School of Social Work and Givat Shmuel dating back to 1969, during which span of time Student Units of both Sequences had generally good learning experiences.
    g. The Local Council's approval of a $50,000 three-year Grant for the establishment, operation, and evaluation of the Learning Center.

The last point "clinched the deal!" In mid-February, 1989, the faculty gave its approval. We spent the second semester setting the framework for the research and operationalization of the Learning Center, and the Center opened with its first group of students in the Academic Year 1989–1990.

Eight groups of students passed through the Center until its untimely demise in 1997. Usually compulsively thorough, I had not thought to check the contract signed between the administrative staffs of the University and the Local Council. In a unique arrangement, no money would exchange hands. Instead, the University would be exempt from paying taxes on the student parking lot situated on Givat Shmuel land. One clause in the contract, however, stipulated that the University could cease the "Project" if the Local Council could no longer fulfill the above arrangement, and if the University could not find alternative funding.

In 1993, unbeknownst to the School of Social Work, the University (and its parking lot) came under the jurisdiction of a larger, neighboring municipality. Thus, the Learning Center and its research component should have ceased to exist. But, in this comedy of errors, the Grant, which had already been renewed once, continued to operate. Thanks to the inability of a computer (and its programmer?) to think, we were able to function until the errors were discovered in 1997. Apparently, the discrepancy between the mid-year start of the Grant and the beginning of the University budget year was not programmed into the computer. So much for serendipity, community planning, and luck!

Key Elements

The next two sections will deal with the operationalization of the Learning Center and the Field Study itself. At this point, however, we would like to emphasize the key elements of our underlying philosophy.

1. The Local Council would fund the Center (according to the contract).
2. The Local Council would provide a building and supportive services for student field work. This would include a classroom for the Community Organization course (according to the contract).
3. The School of Social Work would have full control of the academic program-class and field instruction (according to the contract).
4. There would be a "narrow span of control" of the learning process; i.e., a small, all-purpose staff.
5. There would be "saturation" learning; i.e., reinforcement of core/method-specific concepts via the three Methods courses taught by the same instructor.

6. That same instructor would supervise half the student group, while the other half would be supervised by the agency supervisor. (from now on, we will use the term "Field Instructor" in place of "Field Supervisor"). This would provide "circular feedback" learning which unites rather than dichotomizes class and field.

7. The guiding principle of the Learning Center would be education for Social Work rather than education for Methods.

8. Course content and syllabi would not differ from the rest of the student body. (In practice, the Community Organization course and Field Work assignment did differ somewhat because they were only part of this experimental Sequence as opposed to the full Group Work/Community Organization Sequence. There were other reasons, as well, which we will discuss later).

9. Learning Center students would be together as a group for at least 6 academic hours (and more, as we shall see).

10. Partnership would be the "name of the game"-interdepartmental, University-community-agencies, Learning Center faculty-students, Learning Center Director-Steering Committee.

11. Research would be a sine qua non which would examine as scientifically as possible this field study in social work education.

Operationalization

The Study Grant budget provided for a paid Coordinator of the Learning Center (the Senior author) and a paid Liaison Coordinator from the Local Council (the Director of the Social Services Office). Thus began a nearly round-the-clock, nearly year-round partnership in assuring maximum functioning of the Learning Center. We felt that students and staff should have easy and rapid accessibility to both of us. This included the right to telephone calls until midnight, emergency meetings outside the regular weekly supervisory conferences, and the discussion of individual field problems in class.

In addition, we developed a structured timetable which defined the annual "rhythm of life" of the Learning Center. This schedule was built around the academic year in Israel, which begins approximately October/November (after the Jewish New Year and Sukkot), and ends mid/end June. The following description outlines the timetable and the reasoning underlying each step.

1. May (6–4 weeks before the end of the academic year)-Description of the Learning Center to all First-Year students. In the early years of the Study, this description was given at one of the weekly Class Seminars (a required non-credit Course), attended by the entire First-Year class

(80–100 students). In the latter years of the Study, the Course was eliminated, and we therefore entered each individual section of the Basics Course (4–5 classes of 20–25 students each). Who were "we?" In the first year of the Study (enlisting the first group of students), "we" were the Research Coordinator, the Director of the Social Services Office, and I {who also happened to teach two sections of the Basics Course!). In the remaining years of the Study, students who were about to "graduate" from the Learning Center joined us (voluntarily) on the "description team." These question-and-answer sessions with First-Year students served two purposes. First, students set on becoming caseworkers, but interested in "tasting" community organization, could determine if the Learning Center could fulfill this need.

2. Second, we could identify potential candidates from those who indicated their interest in being accepted as well as those who seemed undecided. Who was a "potential candidate?" Students who asked "challenging" questions, who evinced an orientation toward community as well as individual change, who were open to, and excited about, participating in an experimental program, and who were "passionate" in their desire to burst the Methods confines.

To our pleasant surprise, there was no lack of candidates (although the number varied from year to year, according to circumstances which we will discuss in the Research Section). I invited each candidate to an individual interview, which enabled us to become "better acquainted." Interestingly, some candidates came to their intake interview in couples or small groups of three or four. They were not turned away; instead, I used the opportunity to examine their appropriateness to the intense group learning experience which awaited us, as well as to relate to each as an individual.

More specifically, the student "checked me out" as the faculty member with whom he/she would be spending a great deal of time during the coming year. I tried to test the validity of my first impression (from the Description meetings) of the student's motivation and "openness" and personality. Additionally, however, I inquired about the student's hobbies, languages spoken, general background and First-Year Field Work assignments, and placement preferences (such as types of clients, groups, projects-according to agency, age, sex, and "problem."). I also asked with what other candidates he/she would like to work, if accepted to the Learning Center. Answers to these questions would help me to choose not only the most appropriate individual candidates, but also the most appropriate class composition, and the most appropriate matching of student-workload-agency. Toward that end, I requested each candidate to write his/her answers on a single sheet of paper and rank order his preferences in each of the above categories (e.g. Client Preferences: 1.Child, 2.Young Couple, 3.Middle-Aged Female; If possible, not Older Adult because. . . .), and place it in my mailbox as soon as possible.

I ended the interview by stressing the anticipated hard work in this experimental program, by encouraging any questions the student wished to ask, and by asking him/her if after all this, he/she was still interested. If the answer was positive, I assured the candidate that I would post a list of those accepted within two weeks. My work, however, was still not finished! I asked each candidate's Basics instructor for her/his opinion. The answer to my general question gave me an idea of the candidate's intellectual ability, class participation, and sensitivity to others.

This intake/selection process was expanded somewhat toward the end of the first year (the following May). We invited candidates to visit the Learning Center, to sit in on a Community Organization class, and to get feedback (negative as well as positive) from any of the students in the Center. This approach was consistent with our philosophy of maximum student involvement in the entire shared educational process (the andragogical approach, which we will define and discuss in a later Section).

3. June (First two weeks)-I weighed carefully all the information gleaned during the intake process, and, with perhaps more art/intuition than science, decided on my list. The successful candidates, like all the other students in the School, completed a Field Placement Form, noting their Field Assignment "Givat Shmuel." Unlike the other students, they were not yet assigned a Field Instructor; the Field Work Coordinator permitted me, in cooperation with the other Field Instructor (the Director of the Social Services Office) and the students themselves, to match Field Instructor-Field Learner toward the end of the Orientation period in Givat Shmuel at the beginning of the Academic year. We felt that this would give the students a greater opportunity to know the second Field Instructor, and would give us a similar opportunity to decide which students would "fit best" (personality-wise, learning pattern-wise, and sub-group-wise) with which field instructor.

During these first two weeks of June, I sat for the first time with the Learning Center group, congratulated them on their selection, answered their questions, dealt with their anxieties, and began the process of developing esprit de corps! It was an exciting time for all of us.

4. June (Last two weeks)/July-We met with a variety of agency representatives in order to prepare a preliminary list of agency needs (cases, groups, projects). The Liaison Coordinator and I attended every meeting. In the case of the schools, we were joined by the Social Services Office social

worker assigned to each school. All meetings were held at the agencies themselves. In addition to the schools and the Social Services Office, we met with the nurses at the Mother/Baby Clinic, the Community Organizer, the Director and Community Organizer of the Community Center, the Director of Youth Services, the Coordinator of Drug Prevention Programs, the Director of the Older Adult Club, and the Directors of the Moadoniot (special programs for children from "multi-problem" families).

5. August-I spent this month comparing the lists of agency needs and student preferences. I prepared individual lists of potential cases, groups, and projects. On the individual student sheets, I noted preliminary assignments in rank order under each Method. I also noted which students might be placed together in which agencies and on which projects.

6. September-I prepared special forms for our major source of cases-the Social Services Office-and distributed them to each social worker via the Liaison Coordinator (who also "happened to be" the Director of the Office). He attached a cover letter requesting the completed forms within three weeks in order to allow me to examine them and meet with each worker to determine the suitability of their recommendations. The two-page form contained three sections. The first section-Cases-requested three cases in order of priority (urgency, likelihood to cooperate). The social worker was asked to provide demographic information (Name, address, phone number, age, number of family members), a brief description of the problem, purposes of the intervention, and whether the student would handle the case alone or together with the referring social worker (e.g., the student would work with one of the children and the social worker would work with the parents). The second section-Groups-requested suggestions for two groups, according to type of group (e.g., Friendship, Special Interest, "Therapy"), purpose, potential members. The third section-Community Project-requested a suggested community organization project.

The social work staff generally did an excellent, on time, job of completing the forms, particularly the casework section, and provided an interesting professional connection among the three social work methods. For instance, a Welfare, single-parent mother was suggested as a candidate for individual casework, for participation in a single-parent group, and as a member of a single-parents' self-help group. In practice, therefore, this combination enabled students to understand the single-parent client not simply as a help-taker (Casework) but also as a help-giver (Group Work, Community Organization).

In my meetings with each social worker, we sharpened purposes, dropped or added cases, groups, or projects, and attempted to define in general terms the type of student appropriate to each case, group, or project (e.g. similar in age, similar in sex, temperament/personality). Then, and only then, did I write a student's name alongside each entry in the form. The social workers still did not know the names of the students, and I made my choices on the basis of all the information I had gathered on the students. At this point, I could compare and revise, if necessary, my notations on the Student Sheets and/or the Worker Forms.

7. October/November-The Academic Year begins. We use the first two weeks of Field Work for Orientation to Givat Shmuel. This includes a "gala" opening at the "home base" (a building with bathroom, small kitchen, classroom, and garden), with opening remarks by the Director of the School of Social Work, the Local Council Chairman, the Director of the Social Services Office, and myself. We provide information on the community and its various services, and visit a number of services and neighborhoods on a walking tour. This gives the students (and us!) an opportunity to change Field Assignment choices, if necessary (e.g., a student who preferred not to work with the elderly, changes his mind after our visit to the Older Adult Club).

Between the first and second week of the Orientation, I prepare the "final" List of Field Work assignments, and divide the students according to Field Teacher (here, too, I tried to accommodate student preferences). During the second week of the Orientation, I announce the assignments to the entire group of students. The timing and nature of the workload will be: The first case immediately (the third week of Field Work), the second case no later than the end of the first month of Field Work, the third case the end of the first semester/beginning of the second semester; the first group (already formed) the third or fourth week of Field Work, the second group, preferably "therapeutic" and formed by the student, by the end of the first semester. The Community Organization Project would begin as soon as possible during the first semester.

We expected that at least two cases and one group would be long-term (20–25 meetings). The Project could be individual or shared among two or more students.

In allocating this workload, I attempt to satisfy the first choices of each student, as expressed in their Student Sheets. The students are given the files of their first case (to be read only in the Social Services Office), and summaries of continuing groups and projects. Students are permitted to exchange cases with each other before our final list is prepared. On the last day of the Orientation, the students meet with their respective Field Instructors as a group, and then individually with him.

Meanwhile, back in the classroom, I asked the students in each Methods Course what they wanted to learn, and I utilized the first month to give the students the interventive "tools" to begin their work. Their First-year Basics Course had concentrated more on Casework (e.g. relationship formation, the initial interview, home visits, empathy) in class and field (once a week-two or three cases) than on the other two Methods. Barely two class sessions were devoted to each Method respectively, and in the field, there were no groups, and very rudimentary "projects" (e.g., organizing a holiday party, conducting a Community Survey of a functional or geographic community). A field visit toward the end of the first year did, however, enable the students to see a community organizer in action. The six-hour bloc of time at my disposal-particularly, the back-to-back Casework/Group Work classes-provided flexibility in teaching content.

Thus, I could allocate time in relation to need rather than in relation to rigid Course requirements. This meant initially more time devoted to Group Work and Community Organization theory and practice. This meant teaching techniques relevant to all three Methods (see Sonnheim, 1988, 1995). How, for instance, does one limit an "aggressive" client, group member, committee member? And, most importantly, this meant that the students would experience both a group *and* learning group process (more about this later).

8. December/January-The students are "in process" with their workloads, "crisis management" is shared among the Teachers (Field and Class) and a Student Liaison person to the Social Services Office, and students participate in agency staff meetings. In the field instruction process, we are both demanding and flexible. We demand records in sufficient time to allow us to make written comments and return the records to the students prior to the learning conference. We are flexible regarding type of record-process or summary-although during the first month, we require only process records, in order to help us and the student assess his learning pattern, pace, and needs; and, of course, to prevent "damage" to clients. Thereafter, we give maximum responsibility to each student to decide record type and length of time of weekly learning conference. Interestingly, students did not abuse our flexibility. In fact, their records (both types) became more professional, and, after their initial demands for a continuation of an hour/hour and a half weekly meeting, they used less of their allotted time as their confidence grew. This, too, was consistent with our philosophy of sharing the learning pace with the learner.

In early December, the Liaison Coordinator and I chaired the first of two or three annual meetings of the Steering Committee. We reported on the beginning of the Academic year, dealt with any problems which may have arisen during the intervening months, and shared ideas about future programming. Committee members received an agenda prior to each meeting, and Minutes after each meeting. This was consistent with our philosophy of cooperation and shared responsibility.

9. February-Exam and Evaluation time! All students have a mid-semester break of three weeks for mid-term exams and Field Work evaluations. Classes cease, but Field Work continues. I used the last class in each Course for an evaluation of the Course (had I fulfilled student expectations, and how could I change in the next semester?) Students receive grades in Field Work only at the end of the Academic year. The mid-year evaluation enables Instructor-Learner to set "growth goals" for the second semester, alerts "borderline" students to the need for substantive change, and, in extreme cases, enables the Field Instructor to fail a student. Sometimes, students decide of their own accord that they are "inappropriate" for the profession.

In the Learning Center, the evaluation process takes three weeks. In the first week, the Field Instructor gives the student a copy of the evaluation form, and asks him to make a self-evaluation (verbal, or written, if he wishes) the following week. The Field Instructor does likewise, and the following week they compare notes, and resolve any differences between them. According to our philosophy, if the relationship has been successful ("authentic," "genuine," "open," we believe, are the terms), differences should be small, and there should be no surprises for the student. The Field Teacher then writes the Evaluation, and presents it to the student the following week. If disagreement still exists, the student has a right to attach a statement of his own.

Learning Center students received the same Casework and Group Work exams as students in the Group Work/Casework Sequence, and were not tested as a separate group. Their Community Organization exam did, however, differ in several ways from the exams of the Group Work/Community Organization students. First, the Learning Center students had only a year-end exam. Second, the exam differed from the Group Work/Community Organization exam in style and content. The last class day, I screened a video film dealing with a social problem (e.g. homeless women, prisoner rehabilitation, mental "illness"), asked them to think about the problem in Community Organization terms, told them that there would be specific questions in the written exam, and assured them that they could view the film again during the exam. Needless to say, there was no lack of bureaucratic problems in arranging such an exam for a group of twelve students in an appropriate room for a three-hour period (to allow viewing time), with the required University Proctor "at my side." Interestingly, the open-book exam allowed the Proctor to enjoy the film as well as monitor the students. Third, the exam, like the Evaluation Form for Community Organization Field Work, was geared to students for whom community organization was but one part of their field experience as opposed to the total field experience of students in the Group Work/Community Organization Sequence.

Finally, consistent with our philosophy, the Dean of the School, the Liaison Coordinator, and I met with the students for a mid-year evaluation of their experience in the Learning Center. Criticism was encouraged, and we attempted to change, just as we expected change in our students. Evaluation, for us, was a two-way street!

10. March/April-Class and Field Work continue. The Steering Committee meets again. A Colloqium (e.g., "Citizen Participation in Community Planning") is held in the local Community Center. Two students present their Project. Generally, this is a fairly calm period in the rhythm of life of the Learning Center.

11. May-This month is marked by two parallel and complementary processes of "preparing"-for endings ("termination" sounds deathly final) and for beginnings. The Learning Center students prepared their clients-individual, family, group, community-for ending in a three to four week process. In the first session of that process, the student reminded the client that they would be ending their working relationship by month's end, and that the client should think about what he would like to do in the next three meetings. During the second and third session, student and client try to "finish" "unfinished business," deal with feelings about ending(s) and their behavioral manifestations, and plan "something special" for their last time together. That "last time" may take place in the office, or, in certain cases, a shared ice cream cone outing at the corner store (with a child) or a picnic with a group or a closing party with a self-help group. We dealt flexibly with the famous (perhaps exaggerated) dilemma of gift-taking. What worker should refuse the "gift" of a dozen oranges from the garden of an older adult who wishes to show her appreciation for all she has "received" from the worker? As Field Teachers, of course, we helped the student analyze the situation and stress to her client that there really was "no need" for a gift, and only then, accept it graciously!

The process of ending with the agencies included writing summaries of "treatment" in the individual files of each client, plus completing special Summary Forms which I had devised. These forms would enable me and the agency workers to decide which individuals, families, groups, and projects should continue with the next group of students. These forms enabled us also to "cross index." That is, we were able to determine if an individual client was being served by all three Methods, which Method or combination of Methods seemed most effective, and what was recommended for the future (e.g. immediate transfer to the referring social worker, service "on demand" until "assigned" to another student, no need for further intervention). Clients, it should be stressed, were full partners in this decision-making process, and their reasons for continuing with students instead of with agency social workers were varied and enlightening.

The process of ending with the Field Teachers was similar to the process of the mid-year Evaluation. Only this time, the student received a grade for Field Work. Consistent with our philosophy, we asked the students to grade themselves. In the next-to-last meeting, we compared our grade to the student's grade, and arrived at a final decision (although the Field Instructor had formal authority on grading). The issue of grades was somewhat problematic, as we will discuss later, but we made this shared decision a part of the learning process. If, for instance, a student tended to underestimate his/her ability with a lower grade than ours, the ensuing discussion, and the written evaluation the following week, would help him to value him/herself more realistically.

The process of ending with the Methods classes instructor was a bit more structured because of preparation for the final exams and evaluation of the courses. But this process was tied inextricably to the above processes and to the "preparing for beginnings" process, all of which revolved around me (for better or for worse!) as the Learning Center Director, as the Methods instructor, and as the Supervisor of half the learning group.

We were partners in recruiting and preparing a new group of students-a process similar to that which they experienced the previous May. By month's end, the present group of students had met with the staff of the respective agencies in which they had been placed. Accompanied by the Social Services Office Liaison to each agency, the students and staff evaluated the work experience, and, in many instances, participated in closing ceremonies (e.g., a group presentation at the school, a party at the Older Adult Club).

The process of ending with me and with the Social Services Office culminated with a "festive" Staff Meeting (Eating) which included brief summaries of each student's work (or one or two students' case, family, group, or project presentation). In addition to the Liaison and Research

Coordinators, honored guests were the Local Council Chairman, the Dean of the School of Social Work and his Administrative Assistant, and the Field Work Coordinator. In typically Israeli fashion, each student was presented with a flower and a thank-you-note.

Finally, the students organized their own closing party, either at our "home base" or at the home of one of the students. This small, intimate gathering to which the Liaison Coordinator and I were invited was a moving, fitting climax to an intense shared learning experience!

12. June—For me, the cycle continues. I meet with the Steering Committee to evaluate the current year and to plan for the next. I meet with the new group of students. The process begins anew!

Now, dear reader, lest you think this is just another "show and tell," single-case study, ego trip, Dr. Shlomit Auman Lehman and I will present the scientific aspect of this Field Study in the following Section.

Chapter Two

Research Design and Data Analysis

The main purpose of our study was testing the efficacy of an integrated teaching approach to the social work methods-casework, group work, community organization-combining class and field teaching primarily through one teacher.

The parallel purpose was testing the efficacy of interaction between teaching style and learning style in the learning process and the learning context.

Our independent variable was the learning process which included the principles of andragogic learning, social group work, role theory, and learning theory. An intervening variable was student learning preference.

Our dependent variables were: self evaluation, learning expectation, expectation fulfillment and certification exam grades. We developed 6 hypotheses on which to compare the Learning Center students (learning three social work methods) with two control groups (each learning two social work methods-casework-group work; community organization-group work). The total number of students in each group (for the entire study period of eight years) was:

Experimental Group = 60 (Givat Shmuel-three methods)
Control Group 1 = 285 (Group Work-Casework)
Control Group 2 = 66 (Group Work-Community Organization)

Numbers varied from year to year because of enrollment variations and/or exclusion from totals of students who "dropped out" or who were failed (the number in the Experimental group was very small, 4, and deducted already at the initial count). Numbers also varied according to questions answered on each item in our Questionnaire. The numbers did not include one year during which the Senior author was also on Sabbatical.

The Questionnaire, administered in the first and last class sessions of the year, consisted of two parts. Part 1 contained 6 basic questions, 5 of which required ranking on a 7–point scale. The sixth question was taken from TABS, an instrument developed by the Clinic to Improve University teaching, School of Education, University of Massachusetts at Amherst. The question asked students to indicate their learning style. Part 2 contained 16 multiple choice questions taken from the Study Guide for ACSW Certification (Middleman, 1987). The Before and After Questionnaires are available from the authors.

Unfortunately, there was no pre-test for validity and reliability of the Questionnaire because it would have required a year's use and time was of the essence once the Project was approved.

The following pages present the statistical analysis of the data according to our hypotheses followed by our discussion and interpretation of the results.

The next chapters will then place these results within the framework of andragogy, role theory, learning theory and social work education.

STATISTICS

1. Learning Center students (Experimental Group) will show a higher degree of self-evaluation in their work in all three methods (Casework, Group Work, Community Organization) than non-Learning Center students in the two Control Groups (Casework; Community Organization). (Question A: 1, 2, 3)

In order to examine the differences between the groups on the self-evaluation ratings, six univariate analyses of variance were conducted.

Results of these analyses are presented in Table 2.1. No significant difference was found between the Learning Center group and Group Work/Casework Sequence group groups on the average self ratings of the Ability to diagnose and prepare casework intervention plan ($F(1,341)=2.104$, $p<.148$). No significant difference was found between the Learning Center group and Group Work/Casework Sequence groups on the average self ratings of the casework Ability to intervene ($F(1,340)=1.771$, $p<.184$). No significant difference was found between the Experimental, Group Work/Casework Sequence group and Group Work/Community Organization Sequence group groups on the average self ratings of the Ability to diagnose and prepare casework intervention plan in group work settings ($F(2,370)=0.596$, $p<.552$). Bonferroni post hoc test did not yield significant differences between the groups. No significant difference was found between the Learning Center, Group Work/Casework Sequence group and Group Work/Community Organization Sequence groups on the average self ratings of the Ability to intervene in group therapy settings ($F(2,367)=1.168$, $p<.312$). Bonferroni post hoc

Table 2.1.   Self Evaluation Ratings

	question	experimental		casework		community		
		Mean	SD	Mean	SD	Mean	SD	Sig
Casework	Ability to diagnose and prepare intervention plan	4.86	0.91	5.06	0.95	-	-	0.148
	Ability to intervene	4.81	0.98	4.98	0.83	-	-	0.184
Group	Ability to diagnose and prepare intervention plan	3.92	1.43	4.02	1.39	4.18	1.16	0.552
	Ability to intervene	3.79	1.54	3.89	1.45	4.16	1.10	0.312
Community	Ability to diagnose and prepare intervention plan	3.90	1.49	-	-	4.39	1.28	0.061
	Ability to intervene	3.87	1.57	-	-	4.32	1.37	0.095

test did not yield significant differences between the groups. No significant difference was found between the Learning Center group and Group Work/ Community Organization Sequence group on the average self ratings of the Ability to diagnose and prepare casework intervention plan in community settings ($F(1,114)=3.592$, $p<.061$). Finally, no significant difference was found between the Learning Center group and Group Work/Community Organization Sequence group on the average self ratings of the community Ability to intervene ($F(1,115)=2.826$, $p<.095$).

In order to examine the change in self report ratings of the above variables, Six repeated measures of analyses of variance were conducted, in which the average ratings in each question was used as the dependent variable, and the group variable was used as a between subject factor.

Means and standard deviations of the 'before' and 'after' ratings on the three items are presented in Table 2.2.

Table 2.2.   Self Evaluation Ratings: Before and After

		experimental		casework		community	
		Before	After	before	after	before	after
	question	Mean(SD)	Mean(SD)	Mean(SD)	Mean(SD)	Mean(SD)	Mean(SD)
casework	Ability to diagnose and prepare intervention plan	4.86(0.92)	5.57(0.78)	5.08(0.88)	5.44(0.78)	-	-
	Ability to intervene	4.82(1.00)	5.54(0.79)	4.96(0.82)	5.38(0.79)	-	-
group	Ability to diagnose and prepare intervention plan	3.90(1.45)	5.37(0.96)	3.90(1.39)	3.33(0.94)	4.12(1.15)	5.32(0.89)
	Ability to intervene	3.80(1.56)	5.12(1.04)	3.82(1.53)	5.23(1.04)	4.06(1.14)	5.14(1.00)
community	Ability to diagnose and prepare intervention plan	3.9(1.50)	4.76(1.45)	-	-	4.41(1.28)	5.33(0.95)
	Ability to intervene	3.86(1.59)	4.74(1.48)	-	-	4.29(1.39)	5.24(0.95)

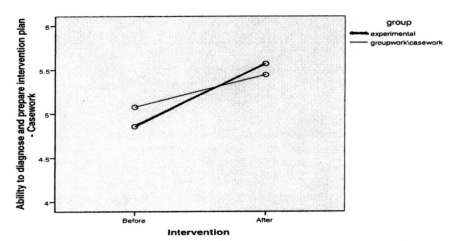

Figure 2.1. Ability to Diagnose and Prepare Intervention Plan: Casework.

Casework

A significant general improvement effect was found between the experimental and casework groups on the average ratings of the ability to diagnose and prepare a casework intervention plan ($F(1,261)=58.616, p<.0001$). In addition, a significant interaction effect was found ($F(1,261)=6.040$, $p<.015$), in which the experimental group, had a significantly larger improvement in the self ratings on this item. This interaction is displayed in Figure 2.1.

A significant general improvement effect was also found between the experimental and casework groups on the average ratings of the ability to intervene-casework intervention ($F(1,258)=52.717, p<.0001$). No significant interaction effect was found ($F(1,258)=2.105$, $p<.148$), in which no significant difference was found in the average self ratings improvement on this item between the groups.

Group

A significant general improvement effect was found between the experimental, casework and community groups on the average ratings of the ability to diagnose and prepare a group intervention plan ($F(1,285)=182.814, p<.0001$). No significant interaction effect was found ($F(2,285)=.586$, $p<.557$), in which no significant difference was found in the average self ratings improvement on this item between the groups.

A significant general improvement effect was also found between the experimental, casework and community groups on the average ratings of the ability to intervene- group intervention (F(1,281)=136.037,p<.0001). Never-theless, no significant interaction effect was found (F(2,281)=.904, p<.406), in which no significant difference was found in the average self ratings im-provement on this item between the groups.

Community

A significant general improvement effect was found between the experimen-tal, and community groups on the average ratings of the ability to diagnose and prepare a group intervention plan (F(1,99)=30.084,p<.0001). No sig-nificant interaction effect was found (F(1,99)=.036, p<.850), in which no significant difference was found in the average self ratings improvement on this item between the groups.

A significant general improvement effect was also found between the experimental, and community groups on the average ratings of the ability to intervene- community intervention (F(1,99)=27.809,p<.0001). Nevertheless, no significant interaction effect was found (F(2,281)=.904, p<.406), in which no significant difference was found in the average self ratings improvement on this item between the groups.

2. Learning Center students will show a greater degree of expectation ful-fillment in all three methods than non-Learning Center students (Before/After Questionnaires; Question D: 1, 2, 3)

3. Learning Center students will show a greater degree of expectation ful-fillment in the community organization course than students in the Casework method Before/After Questionnaire; Question D3).

4. Learning Center students will show at least the same degree of expec-tation fulfillment in the community organization course as students in the Community Organization method (Questionnaire; Question D3). Will the Learning Center students even score higher?

In order to examine the impact of the learning center procedure on the ex-pectation fulfillment of the students, fourteen univariate analysis of variance were conducted in which differences in the average rating of expectations ('before' condition) and expectation fulfillment ('after' condition) were com-pared between the groups.

Descriptive statistics and results of the above analyses are displayed in table 2.3.

Table 2.3. Expectation Fulfillment

subject	subjects question	experimental		casework		community		Overall Sig	Overall Sig
		expectation	fullfillment	expectation	fullfillment	expectation	fullfillment	expect	fulfill
		Mean(SD)	Mean(SD)	Mean(SD)	Mean(SD)	Mean(SD)	Mean(SD)		
method course	Casework	6.10(0.79)	5.53(0.99)	6.11(0.94)	5.01(1.38)	-	-	N\S	**(1>2)
	Group	5.83(1.10)	4.92(1.45)	6.09(1.01)	4.99(1.39)	5.36(1.19)	4.78(1.34)	***(c)	N\S
	community	5.46(1.10)	4.92(1.45)	-	-	5.82(0.96)	5.37(0.88)	N\S	*(3>1)
lecturer	Casework	6.27(0.78)	6.00(0.85)	6.26(0.91)	5.26(1.36)	5.83(0.83)	5.19(1.11)	N\S	***(a)(b)
	Group	6.28(0.89)	4.38(1.20)	6.34(0.84)	5.02(1.68)	5.78(1.38)	4.64(1.43)	*(c)	N\S
	community	6.06(0.87)	5.00(1.56)	-	-	6.22(0.95)	5.26(1.02)	N\S	N\S
professional training		6.32(0.93)	5.73(1.40)	6.45(0.75)	5.48(1.34)	6.07(0.98)	5.28(1.14)	*(c)	N\S

Expectation

As displayed in Table 2.3, an overall significant difference was found between the groups on the average ratings of the expectation in group method course ($F(2,307)=9.287, p<.0001$). A post hoc analysis (Bonferroni) revealed that only the casework control group had a significantly higher average on this variable than of the community control group (Mean Difference=0.73, $p<.0001$). An overall significant difference was also found on the average ratings of the expectation of the lecturer on group studies ($F(2,154)=3.448$, $p<.034$). A post hoc analysis (Bonferroni) revealed that only the casework control group had a significantly higher average than of the community control group on this variable (Mean Difference=0.56, $p<.029$). Finally, the groups significantly differ on the average ratings of the expectation from their professional training ($F(2,306)=4.391$, $p<.013$). A post hoc analysis (Bonferroni) revealed that only the casework control group had a significantly higher average on this variable than of the community control group (Mean Difference=0.39, $p<.011$).

No significant difference was found between the groups on the average expectation ratings of the casework method course ($F(1,263)=0.012$, $p<.913$) and the community method course ($F(1,84)=2.613$, $p<.110$). The groups did not significantly differ in their average ratings of their expectation of the lecturer on casework studies ($F(2,278)=2.516, p<.079$) and in community studies ($F1,39)=0.314, p<.578$).

Fulfillment

As displayed in Table 2.3, a significant difference was found between the groups on the average ratings of the expectation fulfillment in casework method course, in which the experimental group had a significantly higher average ratings (F(1,298)=7.534,p<.006). A significant difference was also found between the groups on the average ratings of the expectation fulfillment in community method course, in which the community control group had a significantly higher average ratings than experimental group (F(1,111)=4.124,p<.045).

An overall significant difference was also found on the average ratings of the expectation fulfillment of the lecturer on casework studies (F(2,309)=8.526, p<.0001). A post hoc analysis (Bonferroni) revealed that only the experimental group had a significantly higher average on this variable than of the group control group (Mean Difference=0.74, p<.0001) and of the community control group (Mean Difference=0.81, p<.017).

No significant difference was found between the groups on the average expectation fulfillment ratings of the group method course (F(2,353)=0.524, p<.592). In addition, the groups did not significantly differ in their average ratings of their expectation fulfillment of the lecturer on group studies (F(2,122)=1.731,p<.181) and in community studies (F1,45)=0.475,p<.494). Finally, the groups did not significantly differ on the average ratings of the expectation fulfillment of their professional training (F(2,346)=1.664, p<.191).

5. Learning Center students will score significantly higher than non-Learning Center students in their answers to Part B (Problems to which to give correct answers).

In order to examine the differences in the average grade of the exam between the groups, two separate univariate analyses of variance were conducted, in which the difference in the average grade in the exams was examined before and after the course. Means and standard deviations of the above analysis are presented in Table 2.4.

No significant difference was found between the groups on the average grade (in percent) in the before the course (F(2,408)=1.142,p<.320). Analysis of the differences in the average grade between the groups, after the course, yielded an overall significant difference (F(2,361)=3.755, p<.024). A post hoc analysis (Bonferroni) revealed that only the experimental group had a significantly higher average grade than community control group (Mean Difference=6.03,

Table 2.4.   Differences in Average Grade of Exam

After			Before			Group
N	STD	Mean	N	STD	Mean	
60	12.91	75.00	60	13.51	70.78	Experimental
246	12.65	73.74	285	13.31	69.75	casework
58	15.52	68.97	66	11.06	67.47	community

p<.040). In addition, the casework control group had a significantly higher average than the community control group (Mean Difference=4.77, p<.041). No significant difference was found between the experimental and the casework control groups. Results are displayed in Figure 2.2.

In order to examine the impact of the course on the improvement in the average grade on the exam between the groups, a repeated measures analysis of variance was conducted. A significant 'improvement' effect was found (F(1,315)=9.489, p<.002), in which regardless of the kind of group, a significant general improvement in the exam grade was found. No significant interaction was found between the improvement and group factors (F(2,315)=2.886, p<.057). Although a trend towards significance was found, there was no significant difference in the improvement on the exam grade between the groups.

6. Learning center students will differ from non-learning center students on patterns of learning preference (more type 1 and 3).

Learning preferences

In order to examine the differences in learning preferences between the groups, ten $\square^2$ crosstabs analyses were performed. These analyses represent five learning preferences items that were given before and after the course. ("Gimel" is Hebrew for "Question C"). See Table 2.5.

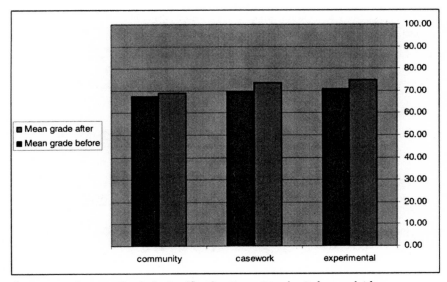

Figure 2.2.   Average Grade in Certification Exam Sample: Before and After.

Table 2.5.   Differences in Learning Preferences (Before/After)

Before

No significant differences were found on Item 1 ($\chi^2(2)$=.743, p<.690).

gimel_bef_1 * group Crosstabulation

			group			
			1	2	3	Total
gimel_bef_1	0	Count	58	293	63	414
		% within group	93.5%	90.2%	91.3%	90.8%
	1	Count	4	32	6	42
		% within group	6.5%	9.8%	8.7%	9.2%
Total		Count	62	325	69	456
		% within group	100.0%	100.0%	100.0%	100.0%

No significant differences were found on Item 2 ($\chi^2(2)$=1.762, p<.414).

gimel_bef_2 * group Crosstabulation

			group			
			1	2	3	Total
gimel_bef_2	0	Count	45	239	46	330
		% within group	72.6%	73.5%	65.7%	72.2%
	1	Count	17	86	24	127
		% within group	27.4%	26.5%	34.3%	27.8%
Total		Count	62	325	70	457
		% within group	100.0%	100.0%	100.0%	100.0%

No significant differences were found on Item 3 ($\chi^2(2)$=1.906, p<.386).

gimel_bef_3 * group Crosstabulation

			group			
			1	2	3	Total
gimel_bef_3	0	Count	24	156	34	214
		% within group	38.7%	48.0%	48.6%	46.8%
	1	Count	38	169	36	243
		% within group	61.3%	52.0%	51.4%	53.2%
Total		Count	62	325	70	457
		% within group	100.0%	100.0%	100.0%	100.0%

No significant differences were found on Item 4.

gimel_bef_4 * group Crosstabulation

			group			
			1	2	3	Total
gimel_bef_4	0	Count	62	325	70	457
		% within group	100.0%	100.0%	100.0%	100.0%
Total		Count	62	325	70	457
		% within group	100.0%	100.0%	100.0%	100.0%

No significant differences were found on Item 5 ($\chi^2(2)=3.969$, p<.137).

gimel_bef_5 * group Crosstabulation

			group			
			1	2	3	Total
gimel_bef_5	0	Count	62	323	68	453
		% within group	100.0%	99.4%	97.1%	99.1%
	1	Count	0	2	2	4
		% within group	.0%	.6%	2.9%	.9%
Total		Count	62	325	70	457
		% within group	100.0%	100.0%	100.0%	100.0%

After

No significant differences were found on Item 1 ($\chi^2(2)=1.435$, p<.488).

gimel_aft_1 * group Crosstabulation

			group			
			1	2	3	Total
gimel_aft_1	0	Count	56	294	60	410
		% within group	90.3%	90.5%	85.7%	89.7%
	1	Count	6	31	10	47
		% within group	9.7%	9.5%	14.3%	10.3%
Total		Count	62	325	70	457
		% within group	100.0%	100.0%	100.0%	100.0%

No significant differences were found on Item 2 ($\chi^2(2)=3.908$, p<.142).

gimel_aft_2 * group Crosstabulation

			group			Total
			1	2	3	
gimel_aft_2	0	Count	45	270	58	373
		% within group	72.6%	83.1%	82.9%	81.6%
	1	Count	17	55	12	84
		% within group	27.4%	16.9%	17.1%	18.4%
Total		Count	62	325	70	457
		% within group	100.0%	100.0%	100.0%	100.0%

No significant differences were found on Item 3 ($\chi^2(2)=4.043$, p<.132).

gimel_aft_3 * group Crosstabulation

			group			Total
			1	2	3	
gimel_aft_3	0	Count	23	165	33	221
		% within group	37.1%	50.9%	47.1%	48.5%
	1	Count	39	159	37	235
		% within group	62.9%	49.1%	52.9%	51.5%
Total		Count	62	324	70	456
		% within group	100.0%	100.0%	100.0%	100.0%

No significant differences were found on Item 4.

gimel_aft_4 * group Crosstabulation

			group			Total
			1	2	3	
gimel_aft_4	0	Count	62	325	70	457
		% within group	100.0%	100.0%	100.0%	100.0%
Total		Count	62	325	70	457
		% within group	100.0%	100.0%	100.0%	100.0%

No significant differences were found on Item 5.

gimel_aft_5 * group Crosstabulation

			group			Total
			1	2	3	
gimel_aft_5	0	Count	62	325	70	457
		% within group	100.0%	100.0%	100.0%	100.0%
Total		Count	62	325	70	457
		% within group	100.0%	100.0%	100.0%	100.0%

Interpretation of Statistics
Hypothesis #1 (Self- Evaluation)

No significant difference was found between Learning Center students and students in the two control groups on all 6 variables of self-evaluation of their work in all three methods at the beginning of the learning process. All students ranked their abilities in mid-range (3–5).

The lack of support for this hypothesis may mean that all students at the beginning of their learning process may, indeed, have a fairly realistic evaluation, neither high nor low, of their abilities.

But, in the two Casework abilities (diagnose/prepare intervention plan; intervene), the Learning Center students exhibited a significant general improvement effect in their self-evaluation of ability to diagnose and prepare a casework intervention plan. They also exhibited a significant general improvement effect in their self-evaluation of their ability to intervene in the casework process. They also exhibited a significantly larger improvement in the self-ratings on these abilities.

In the two Group Work abilities (diagnose/prepare intervention plan; intervene), the Learning Center students exhibited a significant general improvement effect in their self-evaluation of ability to diagnose and prepare a Group Work intervention plan. They also exhibited a significant general improvement in their self-evaluation of ability to intervene in the Group Work process.

In the two Community Organization abilities (diagnose/prepare intervention plan; intervene), the Learning Center students exhibited a significant general improvement effect in their self-evaluation of their ability to diagnose and prepare a community organization intervention plan. They also exhibited a significant general improvement effect in their ability to intervene in the community organization process.

NOTE: Except for the casework ability to diagnose and prepare an intervention plan, the Learning Center students did not differ significantly from the control groups in the amount (interaction effect) of self-ratings improvement on the other five variables. This means that while Learning Center students improved generally in all 6 self-ratings, they shared with the control groups a similar amount of self-ratings improvement in 5 of the 6 variables.

We may conclude, therefore, that the learning process in the Learning Center did increase self-evaluation (and, perhaps, performance). Moreover, their amount of improvement was no worse than students who learned two rather than three social work methods. In Field Work, incidentally, Learning Center students carried approximately the same case- and group-loads as Group Work-casework students. They differed from the Group Work-community organization students who had no cases, one group, and two community organization projects. Thus, the interaction of class and field experience also may have influenced self-evaluation.

Hypothesis #2 (Expectations)

No significant difference was found between Learning Center students and students in the two control groups on their expectations from all three Methods courses, Methods course teacher, professional training.

The expectations of all three student groups (experimental and the two control groups) were consistently high (rankings from 5–6 on a 7–point scale) for Methods courses, Methods course teacher, professional training.

There were, however, significant differences between the two control groups. The Casework control group had a significantly higher average expectation of the Group Work Methods course than the Community Organization control group. The Casework control group had a significantly higher average expectation of Methods course teacher than the Community Organization control group. The Casework control group had a significantly higher average expectation of professional training than the Community Organization control group.

NOTE: Before a post hoc analysis there was, however,

An overall significant difference between the groups on the average ratings of the expectations from the Group Work Methods course.

An overall significant difference between the groups on the average ratings of the expectations from the Group Work Methods teacher.

An overall significant difference between the groups on the average ratings of the expectations from professional training.

NOTE: No significant difference was found between the groups on the average expectation ratings of the Casework Methods course or the Community Organization Methods course. Also, no significant difference was found on the average expectations of the Casework Methods course teacher.

Comparing the two control groups:

The Casework students expected more from the Group Work Methods course than did the Community Organization students.

The Casework students also expected more from the Group Work Methods teacher than did the Community Organization students.

How may we explain this? The Casework students may have "valued" more their two-track (Methods) learning than the Community Organization students, who placed more "value" on their primary track—Community Organization! In practice, for instance, Community Organization students were required only one group (often ill-defined), whereas Case Work and Learning Center students were required two groups. It seems, also, that Community

Organization faculty placed less emphasis on groups than on community projects.

The Casework students expected more from their professional training than the Community Organization students.

This is a bit more difficult to explain, because Community Organization students were generally more "adamant" about their track choice, and were consistently a small (limited by choice and by selection by the Community Organization faculty), "elite" group until the Learning Center three-track system began, and was perceived by Community Organization faculty as competing with them for students.

In addition, Learning Center students who preferred the experimental three-track program were no different from the two control groups in their expectations of learning all three social work methods. We may assume, therefore, that their expectation "investment" in all three methods was distributed more equally than in both control groups.

Hypotheses #3 and #4 (Expectation Fulfillment)

The Learning Center students had a significantly higher average ratings of expectation fulfillment in the Casework Methods course than the two control groups.

The Community Organization control group had a significantly higher average ratings of expectation fulfillment in the Community Organization Methods course than the Learning Center students.

No significant difference was found between the groups on the average expectation fulfillment ratings of the Group Work Methods course.

No significant difference was found between the groups on the average expectation fulfillment ratings of the teacher in Group Work and Community Organization Methods courses.

No significant difference was found between the groups on the average expectation fulfillment ratings of their professional training.

These mixed findings suggest that Learning Center students may be said to be "more satisfied" with their learning Casework than the Group Work-Casework and Group Work-Community organization students. On the other hand, Group Work-Community organization students may be said to be "more satisfied" with their learning community organization than the Learning Center students and the Group Work-Casework students.

All three groups experienced approximately the same degree of expectation fulfillment in the Group Work Methods course.

It should be noted, however, that across the board, fulfillment fell below expectations. That is, while expectation ratings were medium-high (5–6), fulfillment ratings were medium (4–5). This may mean that expectations were unrealistically high, and that fulfillment was an adjustment to reality, rather than just "disappointment."

Considering that Learning Center students had to learn three social work methods instead of two, their expectation- fulfillment ratio compared reasonably well to that of the two control groups. One would expect that casework students would experience greater expectation fulfillment in their major area of learning—casework; and community organization students would feel likewise in their major area of learning—community organization.

Interestingly, the mean difference between expectation and fulfillment on all the variables was smaller for the Learning Center students than for the two control groups.

Hypothesis #5 (Exam Grade)

This hypothesis received heuristic support. That is, although a trend towards significance was found on the improvement on the average grade (Before/After), there was no significant difference between the groups. All three groups improved in the average grade.

A post hoc analysis, however, showed that only the experimental group (Learning Center students) had a significantly higher grade than the Group Work-Community Organization control group. In addition, between the two control groups, the Group Work-Casework students had a significantly higher grade than the Group Work-Community Organization students. No significant difference was found between the experimental and casework control group.

We see from the graph that both before and after the learning process, the Group Work-Community Organization control group scored lower (though not significantly) than the other two groups (experimental and casework).

Hypothesis #6 (Learning Style/Preference)

This hypothesis was not supported. There was no significant difference between Learning Center students and the two control groups.

In the Casework sequence (track), students were not interviewed prior to their enrollment in that track. Thus, there was a random distribution of learning styles. In the Community Organization sequence (track), students chose to enroll, but were interviewed prior to acceptance to the sequence. Some applicants were rejected by the sequence faculty. Thus, there should have been some homogeneity in learning style because of the selection process. This should also have been true for the Learning Center students who, in spite of our very careful selection process, were heterogeneous in their learning styles.

In summary, we may conclude from the statistical analysis that the Andragogic Learning Center did influence self-evaluation and ability to answer correctly certification exam questions in all three social work methods. Although all three groups improved in their average grade after the learning process, the trend toward significance, increased self-evaluation, and significant expectation fulfillment in at least one of the social work methods (Casework), suggests a positive influence of the experimental program.

Basically, learning three methods simultaneously with a limited faculty (one teacher of Group Work, and one teacher of the two methods—Casework and Community Organization) did not affect adversely the students in the experimental group. Nor did the fact that the same classroom teacher of Casework and Community Organization served as well as field teacher for at least half the class in all three methods.

Perhaps we should have anticipated that Learning Center students would share the same beginning self-evaluation and expectations with the students in the two control groups. The more important finding is that, hopefully, because of the experimental learning process, the Givat Shmuel students increased their self-evaluation, experienced higher expectation fulfillment in at least one of the three social work methods, and increased their ability to analyze correctly case examples in all three methods. As a matter of fact, in spite of lower expectation fulfillment in two Methods courses—Group Work and Community Organization—the Givat Shmuel students scored at least as well on the exam as the control group students.

Moreover, their range of learning styles may attest to the ability of the experimental group class and field teachers and the learning process itself to produce students capable of functioning in all three social work methods (at least as shown in the Sample Certification test results). Don't forget, incidentally, that all the students in our study were second-year B.A. students, and they all succeeded on an exam meant for M.S.W. graduates!

Let's now explore the literature relevant to our learning.

Chapter Three

Andragogy

Knowles (1975, 1980, 1984) defines Andragogy as "the art and science of helping adults learn" as opposed to Pedagogy, "the art and science of helping children learn." Merriam (1993) points out that Knowles' later position (from 1970) stressed that pedagogy-andragogy represents a continuum ranging from teacher-directed to student-directed learning, and that both approaches are appropriate with children and adults, depending on the situation. Merriam cites the example: adults who know little or nothing about a topic benefit from teacher-directed instruction until they have enough knowledge to begin directing their own learning. Proponents of this model think that beginning University students need the pedagogic approach (content plan), but as they progress in their studies, the andragogic approach (process plan) is more appropriate. The underlying hypothesis is that adults are independent and thus self-directing. Merriam concludes that andragogy may not define the uniqueness of adult learning, but it does provide a set of guidelines for designing instruction with learners who are more self-directed than teacher-directed.

Knowles (1970, 1984) provides those guidelines in his Andragogical Process Design which includes seven elements:

1. Climate setting
2. Involving learners in mutual planning
3. Involving participants in diagnosing their own needs for learning
4. Involving learners in formulating their learning objectives
5. Involving learners in designing learning plans
6. Helping learners carry out their learning plans
7. Helping learners in evaluating their learning

Caffarella (1993) relates to three principal, but distinct, ideas incorporated into the concept of self-directed learning:

1. It is a self-initiated process that stresses the ability of individuals to plan and manage their own learning.
2. It is an attribute or characteristic of learners with personal autonomy as its hallmark.
3. It is a way of organizing instruction in formal settings that allows for greater learner control.

Caffarella also discusses the philosophical assumptions underlying self-directed learning:

1. Humanistic-The primary guide for self-directed learning. The focus of learning is on the individual and his self-development, with the learner expected to assume primary responsibility for his own learning. Thus, the process of learning is centered on learner need, and is more important than the content of learning. Thus, the educator's most important role is facilitator or guide, as opposed to content expert.
2. Progressivisim-The learner and the learner's experience are central to the learning process. Thus, the learner is primarily responsible for his own learning, and the educator is the guide and encourager. Learning, thus, is practical and pragmatic.
3. Behaviorist-The "how" of self-directed learning. Learners prepare a learning plan (contract) with behavioral objectives, techniques for their attainment, and then evaluate what they have learned.

Caffarella describes two ways of learning-the linear or stepwise process in which the learner identifies his/her learning needs, and then decides which activities, methods, and techniques will be used to satisfy those needs. This process is similar to learning in formal settings.-the trial-and-error process whereby patterns of learning vary from person to person or project to project. Here, the emphasis is on opportunities which the learner finds in his environment or in chance occurrences.

Caffarella proceeds to detail specific stages in the learning process. The first stage is inquiring (a need to solve a problem). The next stage is modeling (observing similar phenomena and developing a prototype model). The third stage is experimenting and practicing (continuous refinement and practice with the model). The fourth stage is theorizing and perfecting (perfecting skills and the product). And the fifth stage is actualizing (receiving recognition for the product of the learning effort). Citing Cavaliere (1992), who used the example of the Wright brothers' process of learning to fly, Caffarella points out that within each stage there are four repetitive cognitive processes, such as goal setting, focusing, persevering, and reformulation, with a clearly identifiable breakpoint between stages, preceded by frustration and confusion on the part of the learner.

One of the major goals of the instructional process is allowing, and, in some cases, teaching adults how to take more responsibility and control in the learning process, i.e., to become an autonomous learner. In some situations, however, adult learners may be "temporarily dependent" (Knowles, 1975) and there are different rates of self-directedness. Caffarella lists four variables which appear to have most influence on whether adult learners exhibit autonomous behavior in learning situations:

1. Level of technical skills
2. Familiarity with subject matter
3. Sense of personal competence as learners
4. Context of learning event

Tough (1979) and Knowles (1975) feel that learner self-direction should be incorporated into organized learning, and learner control, according to Pratt (1988), comes in different forms within that formal setting: ranging from learners wanting the instructor to primarily provide both the direction (what to learn) and the support (ways to go about learning) to learners being highly capable of providing their own direction and support.

Kolb's cyclical model of learning (cited in Wilson, 1993) has four components:

1. Concrete experiences
2. Reflective observation
3. Abstract conceptualization
4. Active experimentation

While Kolb maintains that learning can begin anywhere in the cycle, his model, according to Wilson, clearly has experience as two of its major phases (phases one and four).

A fourth model of learning-the spiral-appears to underly the McMaster model of medical education (Neufeld and Barrows, 1984). The medical student spirals through the same content area several times in the program, each time at a more sophisticated level. For instance, in studying heart and lung problems, the student passes through four phases: introduction to "puffing and pumping;" a model of myocardial ischemia; the mechanisms of cardiac and respiratory dysfunction; direct work with patients with heart and lung problems.

Pratt (1993) suggests a number of ideas for incorporating self-direction into formal instructional settings. One is a step-by-step guide for individual learning plans prepared jointly by teacher and learner. He also presents different models of instruction:

1. A six-step focus on instructor role in which the instructor is involved in identification of learner resources prior to every meeting with the students, and continues with this facilitation role throughout the learning process by helping learners clarify their educational needs, choose appropriate learning activities, and identify useful evaluation strategies. The instructor also fills the more traditional role of content giver and monitor of activities.
2. A four-stage model in which possible instructor roles within each stage vary according to learner's willingness and ability to be self-directed.
3. A nine-step critical practice-learner centered model which stresses the continuous integration of critical analysis and reflection into all but the first step (drafting a learning agreement).

Citing Candy (1991), Pratt emphasizes the difficulty of teachers in shifting locus of control from teacher to learner. The task of facilitator is quite different from telling students what they ought to know and how they ought to learn it. Furthermore, students may not always want or know how to take more control of their own learning, and may actually resent having to participate in this kind of instructional activity. He concludes that fundamental changes in attitudes and beliefs of both teachers and learners about what constitutes formal instruction are needed.

Finally, examining andragogy's contribution to adult learning after twenty-five years (1993), Pratt relates to four questions:

1. What is learning?-In contrast to the behaviorist and empiricist definitions of learning as a change in behavior, andragogy rests on two implicit principles of learning-knowledge is assumed to be actively constructed by the learner, not passively received from the environment; learning is an interactive process of interpretation, integration, and transformation of one's experiential world. These principles are derived from Knowle's five assumptions of self-concept, prior experience, readiness to learn, learning orientation, and motivation to learn.
2. What are the antecedents of adult learning?-Andragogy emphasizes the psychological and individualistic nature of the learner, with his self-concept, prior experience, and perceived needs as antecedents to learning. Thus, the

individual is the "primary reality," the interpretive center of learning and cognition.

3. How can we facilitate adult learning?-The central tenets of the Andragogical Process Design (enumerated earlier) are learner involvement in self-direction. That is, the needs and the experience of the learner take precedence over the expertise of the instructor. The methodology of andragogy is "directed self-directed learning." But the essence of facilitation is not in one's approach as much as in the relationship between learner and facilitator. That is, a relationship, above all, respectful of the individual's freedom from authority and control that might inhibit the natural tendencies of growth and development. Pratt points out that Knowles emphasizes that andragogical approaches require a psychological climate of mutual respect, collaboration, trust, support, openness, authenticity, pleasure, and humane treatment.

4. What are the purposes and aims of adult learning?-Andragogy appears to be based on at least five fundamental values or beliefs: a moral axiom that places the individual at the center of education and relegates the collective to the periphery; a belief in the goodness of each individual and the need to release and trust that goodness; that learning should result in growth toward self-realization of one's potential; a belief that autonomy and self-direction are the signposts of adulthood within a democratic society; a belief in the potency of the individual in the face of social, political, cultural, and historical forces to achieve self-direction and fulfillment.

Pratt concludes, therefore, that andragogy "is saturated" with individualism and entrepreneurial democracy, and societal change may be a product of individual change, but it is not a primary goal of andragogy.

He also concludes that in spite of the widespread adoption of andragogy by adult educators worldwide, it has not been tested and found to be the basis for a theory of adult learning or a unifying concept for adult education. In his view, andragogy may have contributed to our understanding of adults as learners, but it has done little to expand or clarify our understanding of the process of learning. Nevertheless, he stresses that mixed research results on Knowles' process design may derive from an emphasis on studying his methodology to the exclusion of "relationship."

And Merriam (1993), summarizing the Monograph in which many of the above articles appear, points out that a complete theory of adult learning must take into consideration the learner, the learning process, and the learning context.

Chapter Four

Andragogy in Higher Education

Our examination of andragogy in higher education focuses on Merriam's three points-the learner, the learning process, and the learning context.

A. The Learner-The literature on adult learning deals with a range of two to five learning types, patterns, or styles, according to theoretician.

Two-Style-The Goteborg studies (cited in Gardiner, 1989) found two learning "approaches"—the "surface" and the "deep." In the former, students were concerned with remembering the content of a text; in the latter, students were concerned with principles and meaning of the text. Surface approach students may be considered passive learners, while deep approach students may be considered active learners. Pask (cited in Gardiner, 1989) found two learning "strategies"—the "serialist" and the "holist." In the former, students were concerned with memorizing a small section of a fictitious taxonomy; in the latter, students were more concerned with understanding the overall structure of the taxonomy and the hierarchical relationships between sub-species. Gardiner comments that both sets of studies distinguish levels of complexity in learners' conceptions of the learning task, and relates them to stages in the learning process. In addition, he cites Laurillard's (1978) conclusions that learning styles are both content- and context-dependent. Finally, Gardiner (1989, 65) defines "style" as a general cognitive approach, and "strategy" or "approach" to describe how a student tries to learn a specific task.

Three-Style-Building on the above, Gardiner (1989) studied the teaching/learning interactions in social work supervision. He identified three qualitatively different levels of interaction. Level One was associated with a surface-reproductive conception of learning; Level Two was associated with a deep-constructive conception of learning, and a search for meaning through the learner's involvement in the learning. Level Three interactions were characterized by meta-learning-reflection on various approaches to learning, and choosing from a repertoire of approaches to meet the requirements of a task, so that learning to learn enhanced the process of the transfer of the learning. Thus, Gardiner built a three-stage model in which each higher order conception of learning subsumed the one below.

Hokenstad and Rigby (1977) cited Somer's categorization of three major types of learners-the theorist (a deductive approach to learning); the empiricist (an inductive approach to learning); the practitioner (learns by doing).

Meron (1995), in a study of "the good student," found three types of students. The intellectual and talented student was characterized by ability to think analytically and critically, and to differentiate between important and marginal learning material. The diligent and conformist student was characterized by being well-prepared for and never absent from classes. The student who "managed" was characterized by good grades without much effort, and by trying to befriend the lecturer.

Lowy (1978), cites Thelen's three types of learners-the cognitive/rational, the experiential, and the experimental.

Berengarten (1957), in an exploratory study of learning patterns of social work students, defined "learning pattern" as a repetitive selective element found in response to learning demands. He identified three differential patterns of learning-experiential-empathic, intellectual-empathic, the doer.

Four-Style-Navari (1991) points out that Kolb's experiential theory "emphasizes the integration of the abstract concepts of social knowledge with the concrete, subjective experience of personal knowledge." His model, which we discussed earlier, contains four stages of learning which blend in combination to establish four learning styles.

1. Accomodator-Combines concrete experience and active experimentation stages of learning as basis of learning (hands-on experience).
2. Diverger-Combines concrete experience and reflective observation stages. Learns by observing concrete situations, assessing, judging, and brainstorming.
3. Assimilator-Combines reflective observation and abstract conceptualization. Learns by using logic, understanding theory, conceptualizing, and observing.
4. Converger-Combines abstract conceptualization and active experimentation. Learns by searching for problems to fit theories and ideas; he conceptualizes and plans, then tries out his idea. These four styles represent the various ways in which people learn. Where one is located in the circle depends on the individual and the content to be learned. One's ability to utilize all styles is dependent upon the extent to which one is fully indi-

viduated, i.e., the extent to which one has developed his/her cognitive and behavioral skills.

Gelfand, Rohrich, Nevidon, and Starak (1975) used Kolb's Learning Style Inventory in an andragogical application to the training of Children's Aid Society Workers. Although the sample was small, conceptual definitions did not seem sharp enough to us, and a control group was lacking, the findings suggested that experientially-oriented components were more effective than content-oriented components. Please note, however, that Kolb's (1984) four learning styles described above are much more complex (sophisticated?) than his earlier four basic learning "approaches" (concrete experience, reflective observation, abstract conceptualization, and active experimentation) used in this study.

Five-Style-In our study, a question taken from the TABS (Teaching Analysis By Students, School of Education, University of Massachusetts at Amherst, undated), investigated five student learning styles-the cognitive (likes to think for himself), the learner who prefers structure, the learner who likes to share ideas with others, the competitive learner who wants to perform better than others, and the "turned-off" learner who is uninterested in working with teachers or other students. It seems to us that this categorization really adds two new dimensions to learning style range-the lone versus the group learner, and the competitive versus the non-competitive ("turned-off") learner.

B. The Learning Process-Just as there is a range of learning styles, so there are a variety of explanations of the learning process.

Linear-The stepwise process discussed by Cafarella (1993), used by self-directed learners.

Trial-and-Error- (Cafarella, 1993), also used by self-directed learners.

Cyclical-Kolb's model (Kolb 1984; Navari, 1991; Wilson, 1993), which seems to bridge (and perhaps blur) learning style and learning process.

Spiral—The McMaster model (Neufeld and Barrows, 1984), which focuses on the teaching process, but seems built upon the premise that students learn in a problem-based, cognitive, repetitive, increasingly sophisticated fashion.

Intrinsic/Incidental-Hamilton and Else (1983) point out that "Humanists acknowledge the validity of both intrinsic and incidental learning." That is, much human activity is intrinsically valuable; activities are ends in themselves. They cite Pratt's (1976) example of wandering through the streets of Florence, Italy as intrinsic learning. As someone who experienced the streets of that marvelous city for several hours (without a guide book), I can vouch (unscientifically, of course!) for the validity of intrinsic learning. Incidental learning, on the other hand, is "the unintended by-product of learning experiences that had other purposes." We will discuss these two processes more fully in the section on Andragogy in Social Work Education.

Reflective-Boud, Keogh, and Walker (1985, 19) define reflective learning as "a generic term for those intellectual and affective activities in which individuals engage to explore their experiences in order to lead to new understanding and appreciations." According to Schon (1983), this is often a non-technical, non-rational process, where emphasis is on the creative and intuitive, and the learner becomes confident in responding to the unpredictable and unknown. Taylor (1996), citing Boud and Walker (1990) and Boud (1993), points out that "learning from experience can be enhanced through both reflection-in-action, that is, reflection which occurs in the midst of experience, and through reflection after an event (reflection-on-action)." Harris (1996) points out, however, that there is not much discussion in detail of the "reflective nature," and the elements of reflection itself in experiential learning. He suggests that the skill of experiential learning in which people tend to be most deficient is reflection, and that there are identifiable barriers to reflection (in experiential learning). Citing Boud and Walker (1990), he cautions that experiential learning remains a relatively uncharted area with little tradition of research.

Integrative Threading-Lowy (1978), alluding to Bruner's cognitive structuring, discussed "integrative threads" in relation to social work education. He found that "Integrative (rather than fragmented) cognitive learning was more likely to occur when faculty had identified concepts to be learned and had connected them through "integrative threads," that is, frameworks which gave them a structure..." Lowy continues with some examples from social work, such as theoretical formulations (systems theory) or social problems (alcoholism). Burgess (1992) also deals with this learning process in a somewhat different fashion. She cites Holland who argues that it is the difference in style of learning in social work courses that accounts for much of the practice/theory tension. Holland (1989) refers to Bernstein's codes of learning: the collection code in which learning is accumulated like beads on a string, and the integrated code in which new learning is assimilated and prior learning reinterpreted. Interestingly, Lowy, Bloksberg, and Walberg (1971) use the same analog to advance the concept of integrated learning. Citing Bloom (1958), they suggest that separate educational experiences a student may encounter represent large beads on a thin thread.

Imitation (Modelling)-Lowy (1978) quotes Gagne, who states that "learning through imitation seems to be especially appropriate for tasks that have little cognitive structure." Lowy adds that modelling has particular relevance in social work, as many of the aspects of the learning process are more affective than cognitive.

Hierarchical-In regard to cognitive learning, Gagne (cited in Lowy, 1978,17) lists eight types of learning, arranged in a continuum of an hierarchical order, presuming that lower order types are prerequisite to higher order types. Gagne indicates that each higher order of learning depends upon the mastery of the one below it, that it is possible to develop transitions from one level to the next, and that there may well be a kind of spiral development in learning in which the various stages or levels repeatedly assert themselves, but with a different quality of integration as they approach the top of the spiral. The lowest level is signal learning, in which a person learns to make a generalized response to a signal (classical conditioning). The highest level occurs in problem solving, when the learner internally thinks through the combination of two or more previously acquired principles to produce a new capability that depends on a higher order of principles. Some of the intermediate levels include "chaining" of two or more connections and "chaining" of two or more concepts. It seems to us that this process resembles the spiral learning of the McMaster model, the integrative threads of Lowy, and Bernstein's collection and integrated codes.

Both Gardiner (1989) and Taylor (1996) discuss Saljo's (1979) five-level hierarchy of student conceptions of learning. The first three conceptions deal with increase in knowledge, memorizing, and acquisition of facts, whereas the final two conceptions see learning as the abstraction of meaning and as an interpretive process aimed at the understanding of reality. Gardiner views the second and third conceptions as characterizing the passive student (learning is external and something which happens to him), while the last two conceptions characterize the active learner. His three-stage model of learning style (levels of interaction) discussed above is built, in part, on Saljo's study.

Interim Stock-Taking- At this point, we must take stock of the rich, often confusing material presented above. Clarity about the learner-his style and process-will help us facilitate the learning process within the learning context of the University. Thelen's three-style categorization seems most relevant to Higher Education in general and to Social Work Education in particular. These three styles are equivalent to the thinking, feeling, and doing aspects of a learning situation. The learning process itself may be categorized in four distinct ways-linear, trial-and-error, spiral, cyclical. It seems to us that individual style and process, like personality, are part of the developmental history of the child. By the time the individual enters the University, his learning style and learning process have crystallized, and may be identified.

In Table 4.1, therefore, we attempt to show the relationship between style and process. There appear to be clear differences between the learning processes of the cognitive/rational learner and the other two types of learners-the experiential and the experimental. The former is less likely to learn through trial-and-error, and more likely to learn linearly, spirally, and cyclically. True, Kolb's theory is experiential, and defines four "styles," but the cognitive/rational learner may be considered an Assimilator or a Converger because the process of abstract conceptualization characterizes both "styles." In contrast, the experiential, and, probably, the experimental learner learn through trial-and-error. Both seem to learn spirally, sometimes during and sometimes after the trial-and-error process. And both seem to be Accomodators, learning through concrete experience and (or?) active experimentation. Kolb's fourth "style"-Diverger-may characterize both the cognitive/rational and experiential learner.

In Table 4.2, we expand our comparison of the three learning styles, and attempt to show the relationship between them and sixteen variables which appear repeatedly in the literature of learning theory and andragogy. Analysis of the literature leads us to the following tentative conclusion

1. All three learning styles lend themselves to active learning.
2. Nevertheless, hierarchical levels (according to Gagne and Gardiner) differ, with the cognitive/rational learner more likely to attain the highest level.
3. The relationship among learning style, task conception, and content/process orientation seems mixed. The cognitive/rational learner may be less open to process learning and more open to content learning because he prefers a structured learning context. On the other hand, his internal motivation to learn, his level of critical thinking and problem-solving, his deductive approach, his reflective ability, and his self-direction seem to

Table 4.1.   Learning Style and Learning Process

Learner Style	Learning Process			
	1. Linear	2. Trial-and-Error	3. Spiral	Cyclical
1. Cognitive-Rational (2,3,)	X		X	X (3)
2. Experiential (1,2)		X	X	(2)
3. Experimental (1)		X	X	(1,2)

*The numbers indicate Learner Style according to Kolb

Table 4.2. Learning Style and Learning Process: Selected Variable Relationships

Learning Process	Learning Style		
	Cognitive Rational	Experiential Feeling	Experimental Doing
1. Task Conception	DL (2,3)[1]	SL (1)[2]	SL (1,2)[3]
2. Content/Process	C, P[4]	C[5]	C[6]
3. Deductive/Inductive	D (Theorist)	I (Empirical)	I (Doer)
4. Intrinsic/Incidental	Int	Int	Int
5. Threading	Concepts	Experiences	Activities
6. Imitation of Instructor	Thinking	Feeling	Behavior
7. Active/Passive	A	A	A
8. Hierarchical Level	8 (Gagne)	5 (Gagne)	6 (Gagne)
9. Motivation (Internal/external)	I;E	I;E (Feedback)	I
10. Autonomy	Hi	Lo	Hi
11. Control	Lo	Hi	Hi
12. Problem-Solving	Hi	Lo	Lo
13. Critical Thinking	Hi	Lo	Lo
14. Hi (Cognitive)	Hi (Cognitive)	Hi (Feeling)	Hi (How to do)
15. Self-Concept	SD (Self-Directing)	D (Seeks Direction)	ND (Needs Direction)
16. Reflection	IA (In Action; OA (On Action)	OA	OA

Deep Learning Style (Levels Two and Three) Gardiner [1]
Surface Learning Style (Level One) Gardiner [2]
Surface Learning Style (Level One and Two) Gardiner [3]
More Open to Content, Less open to process [4]
Open to Content [5]
Open to Content [6]

characterize a process orientation. Perhaps he needs structure only at the beginning of the formal learning process.

The picture seems a bit clearer for experiential and experimental learners. They seem to be content-oriented, although they learn content through feeling, doing, and trial-and-error. Their task conceptions appear to be Level One and/or Two on the Gardiner scale. They share the internal motivation of the cognitive/rational learner, but the experiential learner, especially, seems to "need" external motivation (feedback) as well. Both the experiential and experimental learners seem to exhibit a lower level of critical thinking, problem-solving, and in-action reflective ability. They differ, however, in their degree of self-direction. The experiential learner seems less autonomous than the experimental learner.

4. All three types of learners display a high degree of readiness to learn, albeit in different ways-thinking, feeling, doing.

5. Their "threading" likewise differs-concepts, experiences, activities.

6. The cognitive/rational learner imitates the thinking processes of his instructor. The experiential learner imitates the feeling processes of his instructor. He learns, for instance, how to listen empathically. And the experimental learner imitates the behavioral processes of his instructor. He learns, for instance, how to assume an empathic posture.

7. The relationship among the four variables-readiness to learn, motivation, autonomy, and control yields some tentative hypotheses which seem to connect learner style and process to learning context. First, motivation seems to be a dependent variable. Thus, degree of motivation varies with degree of readiness to learn and degree of instructor control. Second, autonomy seems to be an intervening variable. Thus, the learner with a high degree of autonomy (self-direction) and a high degree of readiness to learn, will have a higher degree of motivation to learn when instructor control is low. Third, the learner with a low degree of autonomy, and a high degree of readiness to learn, will have a higher degree of motivation to learn when instructor control is high. Fourth, if instructor control is defined as structured learning or the imparting of knowledge, then this variable may have a differential effect on learner style and learner process. The cognitive/rational learner, for instance, may desire structure at the beginning of the learning process, but resent it as the process continues. Or, as we see from Table 4.2, he may desire low control and high autonomy from the beginning. The dilemma of autonomy (self-direction) versus control (structure) underscores the complexity of "directed self-direction" and the pedagogy/andragogy continuum. Candy (1991) stresses that learners may not always want or know how to take more control of their own learning, and may actually resent having to participate in this kind of instructional activity. Lowy, Bloksberg, and Walberg (1971, 158, 159) found that social work students were impatient with the time needed to develop structure. And Wrightsman (1994), discussing the age group 18–22, points out that "young people want autonomy; yet this autonomy is precarious because young people also want safety and belonging, and the comforting assurance that parents will always be there." It seems, then, that this ambivalence continues into the learning context of the University. Let's examine, therefore, Merriam's third point-the learning context!

C. The Learning Context-Burgess (1992), quoting Leftwich, points out that the traditional model of higher education is "inherently conservative and steeped in a tradition of didactic teaching" which may fail to develop critical and independent thinking, or an ability to manage interdisciplinarity. Foeckler and Boynton (1976) stress that "Social work education, like most American adult education, consists of a pattern of structure and expectations that is based on the experience and assumptions of elementary education." Their Notes refer readers to Knowles' discussion of andragogy and pedagogy. They continue their criticizing of higher education, "Because this idea has been extended into adult education, this process is unnecessarily rigid and highly authoritarian." This criticism extends also to those charged with the "education" of the adult learner-the teacher/instructor. In this section, therefore, we discuss Merriam's first two points in regard to the teacher/instructor and the teaching/instructing process.

D. The Teacher (teacher style).

1. The teacher/instructor-Hativa (1995) defines "instruction" as "the activities of the teacher toward students, the results of which will be learning of intellectual content in the area of acceptable social norms, and within a curriculum framework." Within this framework, she continues, "the teacher determines the learning objectives and their order of importance on the basis of his professional knowledge and belief system, values, and perceptions." Teaching, she points out, "is a complex profession, combining aspects of art and science." "Art" includes creativity, spontaneity, and intuition. "Science" includes "deep" knowledge in his area, techniques and strategies for "good instruction." The art of the teacher rests on his personal characteristics, while the science of the teacher can be acquired and improved.

Teacher style is defined by Lewis (1991) as "a consistent arrangement and sequence of elements in a process that imparts to an action or product an unmistakable identity." He points out that "teaching style is manifest more in action than in a product," that "the unique self of the teacher is most clearly manifest in his or her style," and that his (Lewis') intent is to teach students how to learn. Beyond this definition, however, the literature does not present a range of styles as it does for learners. Instead, it deals with continua, dichotomies, power, control, authority, roles, and characteristics.

Merriam (1993), as you recall, points out that pedagogy-andragogy represents a continuum ranging from teacher-directed to student-directed learning. She, too, stresses the art and science of teaching, but, quoting Knowles, distinguishes between the art and science of helping adults learn (Andragogy) and the art and science of helping children learn (Pedagogy). We may conclude, therefore, that there are two basic and opposing teaching styles-the andragogic and the pedagogic. But Merriam adds the time element, noting that adults who know little or nothing about a topic benefit from teacher-directed instruction until they have enough knowledge to begin directing their own learning. The same teacher, therefore, may vary his style in relation to learner need or stage of development. Burgess (1992), defining the teacher as a "facilitator," also views his role as changing over time. In the beginning of the teaching/learning process, he is more active and directive, and by the end of the Course (in Social Work), he is more of a consultant (i.e., less active and directive).

If pedagogy/andragogy is viewed as a dichotomy of teaching styles as well as a continuum, the same may apply to teacher- versus learner-centered learning and didactic- versus non-didactic (facilitative?) teaching. Caffarella (1993), for instance, stresses the importance of learner-centered instruction and critical analysis as key parts of the instructional process. Hokenstad and Rigby (1977), in their discussion of social work education, stress that "didactic instruction creates a situation requiring the student to be a passive recipient of knowledge in the classroom, and, at the same time, an active utilizer of knowledge in the field."

In essence, the above dichotomies may be subsumed under the "knowledge flow direction" of Paulo Freire's "social transformation" curriculum model (Aguilar, 1995) which was designed "to erase the traditional learning concept of knowledge flowing down to students into one in which the learners take responsibility and become the creators of their own learning process."

Change in knowledge flow direction, however, depends upon change in the balance of power, control, and authority between teacher and learner. Kurland (1991) discusses five kinds of teacher power-reward, coercive, legitimate, referent, and expert. Kilpatrick, Thompson, Jarrett, and Anderson (1985), in their case presentation of the andragogical approach to social work education, caution that teachers using this approach must consider the external constraints of the pedagogical model of the University which demands exams and grades. They underscore the subjectiveness in grading. Adelman and Taylor (1977, cited in Hamilton and Else, 1983, 57) observe that power-such as grades and age-used to coerce someone else to behave in ways we (teachers) decide are best is oppressive behavior. Hamilton and Else (1983, 70) seem to go one step further in decrying the power of the social work teacher. Comparing behaviorists and humanists, they attack the rigidity and conformity in competency-based education which tends "to reinforce adjustment of the student to the norms of the majority-competency selected by the established, arrogant, elite powers in a profession-the gatekeepers of tradition-rather than to expand student horizons." We may conclude that power over students, therefore, stems from the profession itself, and that teachers are its socializing agents. Meron's (1995) study of the "good student" tends to support this conclusion. He found that M.A. students' perceptions were closer to those of the faculty (in Humanities, Social Sciences, Medicine) than B.A. students. "Apparently," he concludes, "the longer the student learns in the University, the closer his perceptions to the accepted norms of faculty and administration." The B.A. students perceived the "good student" as diligent and conformist, regardless of faculty. This was probably because most of their time was spent in gaining general knowledge, while M.A. students placed more emphasis on gaining expertise in a specific area.

The teacher's power rests in the locus of control by virtue of the authority granted him by the University. Candy (1991), in his discussion of teacher tasks, emphasizes the difficulty of teachers in shifting locus of control from teacher to learner. He points out that the task of facilitator (i.e., guide, coach, counselor, and/or evaluator) is quite different from telling students what they ought to know and how they ought to learn it. Hokenstad and Rigby (1977) suggest that "In order to achieve a high degree of student participation, the educator may have to relinquish some control over the direction that the discussion takes." That is, the teacher may have to deviate from his lesson plan in response to "related matters" which require discussion. This, of course, is an example of teacher-centered or teacher-directed learning versus student-centered or student-directed learning.

The classroom teacher, according to Kurland (1991), should, therefore, be an authority, but not authoritarian. His authority should derive from his knowledge of the subject matter, but, as Hokenstad and Rigby (1977) point out, he should be a facilitator of learning rather than just a knowledge transmitter. They add that he must also possess an understanding of how students learn, and a teaching strategy that engages the student.

How, then, may we summarize the role of the teacher? Role theory, which "concerns the study of roles, or patterns of behavior that are characteristic of persons and contexts" (Biddle, 1979, 20), provides a framework for the systematic examination of teacher-learner roles and the interaction between them. Biddle points out "that teaching involves role behaviors on the part of both teachers and pupils, and that teaching goes on within a context of demands and beliefs," and thus, "it is possible to view much of education within a role framework." He provides a rich glossary of 334 key terms and concepts, a fraction of which we will use to sharpen the often imprecise and varying definitions of teacher/learner roles in the literature.

Defining role as "those behaviors characteristic of one or more persons in a context," Biddle stresses that "This definition hangs on four terms-behavior, person, context, and characteristicness." Thus, roles are behavioral, they are performed by persons in a specific context, and consist of those behaviors that are characteristic of a set of persons and a context (1979, 58). A fifth concept-task-"refers to shared intentions for activity that appear within the system (whether or not they are accomplished)."

These concepts provide us with a more solid basis for examining the role, task, and behavior of the teacher/instructor in the context of the University. In Table 4.3, therefore, we present our taxonomy of major teacher roles, the tasks within each role, and the characteristic behavior required to perform those tasks. The letters "A" and "P" indicate whether the role is primarily andragogical or pedagogical. Both letters before the role indicate that the approach depends on teacher style and/or timing.

The asterisk* indicates that the role is also that of "Supervisor" and will be discussed more fully in the pages dealing with field teaching.

The literature reviewed above describes at least seven major teacher roles. Four roles (Facilitator, Resource, Model, Group Worker/Mediator) are clearly andragogical. Three roles (Content Expert, Socializing Agent/Gatekeeper, Monitor of Activities) may be pedagogical and/or andragogical, depending on teacher style, timing, and context (University) demands.

The most frequently-mentioned role is facilitator (Burgess, 1992; Caffarella, 1993; Candy, 1991; Foeckler and Boynton, 1976; Hokenstad and Rigby, 1977; Graham, 1997; Kilpatrick, Thompson, Jarrett, and Anderson, 1984; Knowles, 1972; Kurland, 1991; Pratt, 1993; Rothman 1973; Taylor, 1996). Obviously, this is the teacher role most preferred by supporters of andragogy. This role "colors" all the others. The facilitative teacher uses his content expertise selectively, and as a stimulus to discussion and (even!) disagreement. He is a "resource" to resources; a model of thinking, feeling, and doing; an "introducer" to the values, knowledge, and techniques of the profession; a stimulus to peer learning; and a partner in learner evaluation.

The non-facilitative teacher (pedagogue?), on the other hand, uses his content expertise to provide the learner with the knowledge which he, the teacher, thinks ought to be learned. He does not stimulate peer learning among the passive recipients of his expertise. He utilizes exams and evaluations to determine if the "ought-to-be-learned" has indeed been "learned," and uses grades as a "gatekeeping" device. Obviously, these are the teacher roles least preferred by supporters of andragogy.

2. The teaching/instructing process-It seems to us that just as teacher styles and roles vary, so does teaching process. This we can only infer from

Table 4.3.   Teacher Role

	Task	Behavior
1. Facilitator (A)	1. Increases motivation to learn. 2. Creates learning climate*. 3. Involves learners in mutual planning. 4. Involves learners in diagnosing their own learning needs. 5. Involves learners in formulating their learning objectives. 6. Involves learners in designing learning plans 7. Involves learners in evaluating their learning. 8. Develops learning process* 9. Develops problem solving ability* 10. Provides learning framework* 11. Clarifies educational needs.* 12. Helps learner acquire skills*. 13. Develops open expression of feelings* 14. Develops self-direction	1. Relates* 2. Gives Feedback* 3. Positive* or Negative reinforcement. 4. Counsels 5. Guides* 6. Encourages* 7. Evaluates*
2. Content expert (A;P)	1. Increases knowledge (In Social Work skills, techniques and values	1.Transmits knowledge* 2. Transmits technical skills*.
3. Resource (A)	1. Increases ability to use resources 2. Increases self-direction	1. Identifies and directs to resources.

4. Model (A)	1. Develops professional behavior and values (cognitive, affective, and experiential behavior	1. Reflects*
		2. Analyzes "threads"
		3. Expresses feelings*
		4. Role Playing*
		5. Listens empathically*
		6. Empathic posture
5. Group Worker/ Mediator (A)	1. Encourages learner interactions (with each other), i.e., increases learning through group interaction*	1. Enables
		2. Listens
		3. Clarifies*
		4. Draws out
		5. Guides*
6. Socializing Agent/*Gatekeeper (A;P)	1. Prepares learner for entrance to profession	1. Coaches*
		2. Transmits values
7. Monitor of Activities (A;P)	1. Assures "adequate" performance	1. Grades
		2. Evaluates*

* indicates supervisor or teacher role

the literature on the learning process, since "teaching process" seems undifferentiated from "teaching style" (more on this later). Linear teaching, therefore, seems to us a process suitable to linear learners (Caffarella, 1993), and utilized, probably, by pedagogic, content-oriented, didactic, teacher-centered, directive teachers. Trial-and-error teaching seems less likely in a classroom context. However, the andragogic, process-oriented, non-didactic, student-centered, non (less)-directive teacher may, in fact, encourage students to solve problems through trial-and-error thinking in order to facilitate learner self-direction. This process may be less suitable for cognitive-rational learners. Spiral teaching exemplifies the McMaster and hierarchical models of Gagne, Gardiner, and Saljo. The former seems appropriate for all styles of learners, while the latter may be more appropriate for different styles at different levels. We think that the andragogue adapts this process to the different learning styles in his class, whereas the pedagogue "spirals" ahead undifferentially. Kolb's cyclical model, although basically experiential, requires an even finer differentiation-among four learning styles. We will discuss this further when we examine teacher-learner interaction in light of role theory and research findings.

In addition to, or perhaps within the framework of, the above four basic teaching/learning processes, may be grouped intrinsic, integrative, and modeling/reflective teaching. The intrinsic teacher "wanders through Florence," so to speak, with his students. That is, the very process of shared problem-solving is a learning experience in itself. This process may be more suitable for experiential and experimental learners than for cognitive/rational learners. The integrative teacher "threads the beads," so to speak for and/or with his students. And, as Lowy, Bloksberg, and Walberg (1971) point out, the "integrative thread could be conceived as consisting of any idea, framework, problem, method, or device by which two or more separate learning experiences are related." Thus, this process is suitable for all learning styles, although the framework orientation may seem more appropriate for linear learners (cognitive/rational style). The pedagogic teacher may tend to thread "for," while the andragogic teacher may tend to thread "with" (or perhaps "for" at the beginning of the process.). Finally, the modelling/reflective teaching process may, indeed, encompass all the aforementioned processes. The teacher serves as a role model for the learning process. The student may imitate his thinking, feeling, doing processes-the way he "threads," for instance-and thus adapt his own learning processes to those of the teacher. The andragogue, reflecting in- and on-his classroom problem-solving "teaches" reflection by example rather than by lecture.

3. The interaction between teacher and learner-Teaching and learning are not, however, mutually exclusive, one-way processes. The interaction between teacher/instructor and student/learner (or group of student learners) influences both parties to the interaction. If "education is a personal change process" (Hamilton and Else, 1983), if "learning requires change" (Foeckler and Boynton, 1976), and if we wish the learner to choose "to assume the primary responsibility for planning, carrying out, and evaluating those learning experiences" (Caffarella, 1993), we must examine that interaction in more depth. Role theory helps us to do so.

In Table 4.4, we have listed role concepts relevant to teacher/instructors and role concepts relevant to the interaction between them and student/learners. Some concepts (such as, authority or formality of an expectation) appear in both lists because they are relevant to both teacher and learner as well as to the interaction between them. Definitions of each concept appear in alphabetical order in Biddle's Glossary (1979, pp. 381-397). We have attempted to group these concepts in a way which highlights the pedagogy/andragogy dichotomy/continuum, as well as examine the somewhat limited research on teacher/learner role interaction.

Teacher concepts may be grouped into six major categories. The first c ategory-Teacher Position-includes the concepts of socializing agency, contextual role, formality of expectation, authority, prestige, power, treatment, and

Table 4.4.   Role Concepts: Teachers/Learners

	Teachers	Learners
1. Teacher Position	1. Socializing agent	A. Individual
	2. Contextual Role	1. Anticipatory Socialization
	3. Formality of expectation*	2. Readiness to learn
	4. Authority*	a. own position
	5. Prestige	b. personal expectations
	6. Power	c. expectations for self
	7. Treatment	d. expectations for others
	8. Influence	e. self-role congruence
		3.Characteristics
		a. Characteristicness
2. Model	9. Modeling*	b. Contextual role
	10. Charisma	c. Formality of expectation
3. Role	11. Coherence	d. Target
	12. Self-Role congruence	e. Recipient person
	13. Role Ambiguity	4. Conflict
	14. Role Conflict	a. Value and role conflict
	15. Role Distance	B. Group
		1. Group
4. Span of Control	16. Span of control	2. Behavioral contagion
5. Empathy	17. Empathy*	
6. Facilitation	18. Facilitation*	

* indicates supervisor or teacher role

influence. The socializing agency is the University which circumscribes teacher behaviors by formal expectations of role performance. Thus, the University bestows upon its position occupants (the teachers) authority, prestige, power, and influence-"behaviors characteristically directed toward persons in a context" (i.e., treatment, Biddle, 1979, 62); namely, the students.

The second category-Model-includes the concepts of modeling and charisma. The teacher may serve as a model with whom the student/learner may identify, and thus imitate. "Modeling may or may not be consciously engendered, but in either case, it results in the person taking on the behaviors characteristic of the other-that is, his or her role" (Biddle, 1979, p. 45). The charismatic teacher, like the charismatic leader, "has certain personal mannerisms that appear in the behaviors of his or her followers" (in our case, students) (Biddle, 1979, p. 45).

The third category-Role-includes the concepts of coherence, self-role congruence, role ambiguity, role conflict, and role distance. A research-oriented teacher may experience difficulty in performing his teaching role (lack of coherence).A beginning teacher (Teaching Assistant, Lecturer) may experience a lack of congruence between his personal characteristics and his expected role. As Biddle points out, "New entrants into positions normally face a period of adaptation and learning before they can perform roles adequately." (Biddle, 325). Role ambiguity can make that adaptation more difficult, and role conflict can exacerbate it even more. If, for instance, the University does not clarify desired teacher behavior and its time and value allocation (teaching versus research/ publication), role ambiguity occurs. Role conflict, however, occurs when the University demands research/publication, but the students demand teaching. In the former, the teacher lacks clear guidelines about what to teach, how to teach, and what should be the finished product of his teaching (a self-directed learner?) In the latter, the teacher is caught between conflicting role expectations about what to stress in class (intra-role conflict) or research/publication versus teaching (inter-role conflict). Role Distance deals with the degree of teacher involvement with his student/learners. "Involvement" may run the gamut from permitting students to address us by our first names to dealing with personal problems to having sex. Beginning teachers may mask their lack of confidence by being too formalistic (pedagogic?) or too "open" (andragogic?).

The fourth category is Span of Control. This refers to "the number of persons over whom a given leader has authority" (Biddle, 269). If we apply this concept to the teaching/ learning context, we may make a number of assumptions. First, the larger the class, the greater the difficulty the teacher may experience in asserting his authority and control (not to mention his difficulty in remembering names!). Second, the more students, the greater the variety of role expectations. Third, the larger the class, the greater the possible role distance, the lesser the likelihood of "involvement," and the greater the likelihood of "selective involvement" with students whose learning process and style resemble those of the teacher.

The fifth category is Empathy. Biddle's discussion of the concept (186–189) questions whether empathy is a single trait or whether it consists of different components. Nevertheless, he does point out that if, indeed, some people are "better judges of the thinking of others" (i.e., have more empathy), "such persons would surely make better group leaders, counselors, therapists, or confessors." He seems to prefer the concept of role taking—the ability to take the role of another. Persons with this ability can then predict and understand the other's reactions in various situations. Needless to say, a teacher, particularly an andragogic one, should be empathic and capable of role-taking.

The sixth category is Facilitation. According to Biddle (1979, p. 38), "A given behavior facilitates or hinders another behavior if it relocates or deforms an environmental unit in such a way as to raise or lower the probability of eliciting the latter." At first glance, Biddle's analysis of the concept seems to contradict the "enabling" function of facilitation stressed in the andragogy literature. He raises the possibility that a human being may be an "environmental unit" which may be manipulated ("relocated" or "deformed"). But his citing of facilitation as one type of behavioral linkage, and his example of husband-wife "mutual facilitation" (Biddle, 1979, pp. 37–39), does, in fact, provide a clearer conceptual, and, perhaps, possible operational definition of the facilitator role. There is, indeed, a linkage between teacher-learner behaviors which occur in the learning context. This brings us to an analysis of the learner and interactive concepts which appear in Tables 4.4 and 4.5. Learner concepts may be divided into two sets of categories-Individual and Group. In the first set, we suggest four major categories.

The first category-Anticipatory Socialization-refers to a person anticipating his entrance to a new position by adopting aspects of its role prior to assuming membership. The young adult accepted to University, for instance, begins to walk, talk, and dress like a University student (see the TV series, "Felicity"). The learner for a profession (like Law, Medicine, Education, Social Work) adopts the external accoutrements of his future profession ("legal lingo," empathic posture) even before their internalization. There is, thus, a readiness, positive, albeit sometimes exaggerated, for the next step in the personal change process.

The second category-Readiness to Learn-includes the concepts of own position, personal expectations, expectations for self, expectations for other, and self-role congruence. The reality of occupying (instead of simply anticipating) the position of student/learner entails expectations for self and others. The "others" are fellow students and teachers (see Biddle, 1979, Table 5.1, 125). The new student, like the new teacher, should possess a high degree of self-role congruence in order to adapt to his new position. This combination of self-role congruence, expectations for self and others, preceded by anticipatory socialization, seems to us a positive indication of readiness to learn.

The third category-Characteristics-includes the concepts of characteristicness, contextual role, formality of expectation, target, and recipient person. As Biddle (1979, 58, 59) points out "Roles consist of those behaviors that are characteristic of a set of persons and a context." Thus, we may say that the characteristic role of students involves learning. The University setting provides a context for his role performance (although we know from the literature that learning, particularly self-directed learning, also occurs outside formal educational settings). The University, and the teacher as its representative, sets formal, often written in great detail, expectations of student/learner behavior. Similar written expectations of teacher behavior seem strikingly absent. The student, who is both target and recipient person of teacher behavior thus may be affected differentially by a pedagogic, as opposed to an andragogic, teacher.

The fourth category-Conflict-includes the concepts of value and role conflict. Biddle, in his discussion of the person in a social context raises two points particularly relevant to the student/learner in our thesis. "The youth (no longer a child) should learn that internalized expectations are not inviolate. . . . In Piaget's terms, the youth should now become autonomous." (Biddle, 1979, 294). "The adult (no longer a youth) should learn how to change and control the features of the social systems in which he or she participates. . . . The self is no longer a passive accommodator, but is now conceived as a social planner and doer." (Biddle, 1979, 295). In andragogic terms, therefore, the young adult student is an autonomous, active learner who should be able to influence the learning context of which he is a part (i.e., the University and its representative, his/her teacher). Like the teacher, however, the student may experience role conflict. Is he a "student" (passive learner), or is he a "young adult" (autonomous, self-directed learner)? As a student, are different expectations of his behavior held by his teacher and his peers (fellow students)? The former conflict is inter-role, while the latter conflict is intra-role. Both, as we shall see, influence learner/teacher interaction.

In the second set of learner concepts-Group-we suggest two categories. The first category is Group, defined by Biddle as "a set of two or more persons who are linked through interaction." (Biddle, 1979, 233). He then defines interaction as "a condition existing between two or more persons such that each exhibits one or more behaviors which affects the other(s) during the period of our observation." (Biddle, 1979, 233). These definitions may apply to a group of students in a classroom context-a "learning group" in andragogical terms-or to the individual/multiple interaction between that group and the classroom teacher. If that teacher is an andragogue (or a Social Work instructor with group orientation), he may be an integral part of that "learning group" (more on this in the section on Andragogy in Social Work Education).

The second category is Behavioral Contagion, defined by Biddle as "imitation wherein the mechanism operative is reduction of expected sanctions that normally restrain behavior" (Biddle, 1979, 44). This definition, and the treatment literature cited by Biddle, projects a negative connotation to the concept. In contrast, we believe that behavioral contagion can also be positive in the learning context. The andragogue can allow or facilitate behavior not normally sanctioned in the classroom situation. For instance, the entire group of students may disagree with him (spurred on by one brave soul!), or the entire group may

Table 4.5. Teacher/Learner Interaction

1. Behavioral Linkage
    a. Facilitation /Hindrance
    b. Reward/Punishment
    c. Reinforcement (Positive/Negative)
    d. Imitation (Behavioral Contagion; Behavioral Conformity)*
    e. Modeling*
    f. Influence (Sanctions (see especially, p43 in Biddle); Power)*

2. Roles
    a. Role Complementarity; Role Reciprocity
    b. Treatment Sector
    c. Role casting
    d. Contextual Role

3. Role Expectations
    a. Role Expectations
    b. Expectations
    c. Assumption of Conformity
    d. Assumption of Sanctioning
    e. Assumption of Simple Formation
    f. Object Person/Subject Person
    g. Expectation for Self
    h. Expectation for Other

4. Expected Roles
    a. Expected Role
    b. Expected Treatment

5. System
    a. Structure (Authority Structure)*
    b. Relationship*

*Indicates supervisor or teacher role

emulate one or two self-directed, reflective learners, or the entire group may "limit" a "destructive" student (more on this later.).

Now that we have examined teacher and student concepts, we may examine the interaction between them. Interaction concepts may be divided into five major categories. The first category is Behavioral Linkage. Biddle points out that "two behaviors are said to be linked if the performance of the first affects the probability of the performance of the second." (Biddle, 1979, 37). Although Biddle notes that behavioral linkage is defined as a one-way process, he adds that "Nothing whatsoever is said about the possible effects of the behavior of the other upon subsequent behavior by the person." Thus, in our andragogic application of this concept, the teacher (Person) may also be affected by the behavior of the student (Other). Biddle also notes that "if the person's behavior alters the probability of behavioral elicitation in the other, it must either increase or decrease that probability." (Biddle, 1979, 37). This, too, has implications for the andragogic/pedagogic dichotomy/ continuum, as we shall see.

Biddle's division of Behavioral Linkage concepts into Simple and Complex is not completely clear to us. Apparently, simple linkages are straightforward one-way processes, whereas complex linkages, while also one-way processes, involve the co-occurrence of other processes. We have chosen three simple and three complex concepts which seem relevant to teacher/ student interaction.

The first category-Linkage-includes the three simple concepts of Facilitation, Reward, and Reinforcement, and the three complex concepts of Imitation, Modeling, and Influence.

"Facilitation occurs when one behavior affects another by means of environmental manipulation" (Biddle, 1979, 38). According to Biddle, facilitation occurs when one behavior increases the probability of another, whereas, hindrance occurs when one behavior decreases the probability of another. Citing husband-wife behavior, Biddle (p. 38) notes that "it is possible to discover behaviors of the person and the other so that they facilitate one another." Thus, behavior may be "mutually facilitative." It seems to us, therefore, that the concept of facilitation is more complex than it seems. A number of questions arise if we apply the concept to teacher/student interaction in the learning environment. First, what constitutes facilitative teacher behavior? The pedagogue may indeed "manipulate" the learning environment in a one-way didactic process. The andragogue, however, may "facilitate" the learning environment in a two-way mutual process. Biddle's example of two men on the opposite ends of a long cross-cut saw (38) is most appropriate. Teacher and student may facilitate or hinder the learning process "depending on whether or not they can pull in alternating rhythm." Second, can teacher hindering behavior be decreased by student facilitating behavior in the learning situation (or vice versa)? Third, can there be "mutual hindering?" Fourth, how do class size and student learning style affect facilitation/hindrance? We will attempt to answer these and other learning context questions in the section which deals with research.

"In contrast with facilitation, rewards are presumed on a basis of behavioral prepotency" (Biddle, 1979, 39). These are "behaviors whose force is so great that no human being receiving them and having normal facilities can be other than aware of them." (Biddle, 1979, 35). According to Biddle, facilitation is mediated through environmental manipulation, while rewards and punishment are assumed to be induced through motivation, even if the target of the reward or punishment provides no recognition response. In the case of teacher/student interaction, a "good" grade in a paper or exam should be rewarding (bring pleasure) to the learner and increase his motivation to learn, whereas a "poor" grade should be punishing (bring pain) to the learner, but also increase his motivation to at least "do better" next time. We agree with Biddle that this process is more complex than it appears, although research shows that people tend to choose behavior which maximizes reward and minimizes punishment. In the learning situation, for instance, a "poor" grade may indeed decrease motivation, whereas a "good" grade may not necessarily increase it. The "good" student may evaluate himself in relation to his own standards and past performance as well as in relation to his fellow students. Thus, his definition of a "good" grade may differ from the teacher's definition (and this, too, may vary with the "toughness" of the teacher as a grader.). In addition, teacher type may influence the type of learner rewarded. The pedagogue, for instance, may reward the passive learner more than the self-directed learner. The andragogue, however, may vary his rewards to suit individual learner type, with the ultimate goal of increased motivation toward self-directed learning for all students.

Reward and punishment is also a two-way process. As student grades improve, teacher satisfaction should increase (even for the pedagogue!). The "tough" ("unfair?") teacher can be "punished" by the class as a group with a variety of sanctions ranging from mass boycott of class sessions to formal complaint to the administration. A "tough" but "fair" teacher, however, may be rewarded by class respect and increased motivation to meet his or her particular standards.

Reinforcement, which "occurs when one behavior enhances or decreases the probability of another through recipience" (Biddle, 1979, 393), differs from reward in three ways. First, reinforcement is situationally specific; i.e., "those stimuli which reinforce one person positively (increase the probability of the other's response) may reinforce another negatively (decrease the probability of the other's response) and provoke no response at all in a third" (Biddle, 1979, 41). For instance, a teacher's questioning comments on student papers may stimulate some students to "try harder" (positive reinforcement) and other students to "give up" (negative reinforcement). Second, "many behaviors that reinforce responses in another would not normally be considered to constitute reward or punishment." (Biddle, 1979, 41). For example, lowering a student's grade for late submission of a paper, may, indeed bring more of the same with future papers. The student may respond with anger or fear, thus delaying rather than submitting on time. Third, the person providing the stimulus must first define the desired response before deciding whether the reinforcement should be positive or negative. For instance, if the classroom teacher wishes to decrease passive learning, should he reduce positive reinforcers (such as "frontal" lectures) or increase negative reinforcers (such as group discussions)?

This concept, like the above two linkage concepts, can be mutual. The individual learner, and perhaps even more effectively, the learning group, can reinforce desirable teacher behavior by consciously or unconsciously providing positive or negative stimuli (such as increasing initiative for classroom discussion-a negative reinforcer for "frontal" lecturers).

Imitation, the "simplest" of the complex linking concepts, involves the co-occurrence of two processes-correspondence and linkage. "A behavior will be said to imitate another if it is linked to and corresponds with the other." (Biddle, 1979, 44). Normally, imitation results from the interaction of Person and Other, but an individual may imitate himself, especially if his behavior is rewarded (reinforced?) by others. It seems to us that imitation is more a one-way than a two-way process. In the learning situation, for instance, it is more likely that students will imitate their teachers rather than vice-versa. The andragogue may influence (consciously or unconsciously) his students to "imitate" his thinking, feeling, doing, reflecting, "threading." Moreover, the individual student in such a learning situation may experience a process of imitating his teacher, his peers, and then himself. Thus, there is a "snowball" effect of self-directed learning. The andragogue, however, does not wish a class of robots. Therefore, he/she encourages differential imitation, according to individual student learning style, within the general framework of self-directed learning.

Modeling, according to Biddle, is "yet another term used for imitation." (Biddle, 1979, p. 45). Consciously or unconsciously, Other (the student) models his behavior on Person (the teacher) with whom he identifies. The student exhibits the behaviors of his teacher. In essence, therefore, the andragogic teacher "causes" social facilitation (another term for imitation), behavioral contagion, conformity (in its positive sense), imitation, and modeling in order to "cause" self-directed learning. By contrast, the pedagogic teacher may stifle such learning, utilizing the same five concepts, but with different results, i.e., passive learning.

According to Biddle, "a person influences another when the person's behavior affects one or more behaviors of the other and we have evidence of advertence on the part of the person" (Biddle, 1979, p. 389). This means that there is a conscious attempt by one person to affect the behavior of another, through direct injunction, indirect injunction, nonverbal injunction, and sanctioning. These forms of influence are quite relevant to teacher/learner interaction. A full range of teacher behaviors, conscious or unconscious, overt or expectational, "influence" (change?) student learner behaviors. For instance, course requirements, teacher demands, exams, evaluations, grades, smiles, grimaces relay messages to students about how they should behave. Students who conform to teacher demands tend to receive good grades, while students who do not conform, tend to receive "bad" grades. The teacher, whether he is an andragogue or a pedagogue, tends to "shape" students in his image. This is not necessarily negative! The problem arises when the teacher does not relate to individual learning style, and "shapes" an entire class into passive learners. Such a teacher is merely a gatekeeper, in our estimation. Moreover, Biddle, notes that "sanctioning characterized much of the pedagogy to which we were exposed during our early school years…" (Biddle, 1979, p. 218). He discusses at length the related concepts of sanctions (positive and negative), reward and punishment, reinforcement, power, authority, and charisma. He concludes that sanctioning is one of several strategies for "organizing" behavior. He notes also that the assumption that "object persons conform in their behavior to role expectations because of sanctioning they are exposed to or because they anticipate the imposition of sanctions from others supporting conformity . . . is not generally needed and may be in error for many forms of interaction." (Biddle, 1979, 217).

The implications for teacher/learner interaction are many. In the case of a "deviant" student, for instance, the pedagogue may "make an example" of him by sanctioning his behavior, whereas the andragogue may encourage the "deviance" as an example of individual learning style. But even the andragogue may sometimes need to limit disruptive/destructive behavior. He differs, however, from the pedagogue because he may enable the learning group to exercise influence rather than use only his authority. In other words, he shares power with the students. The andragogue may exert influence by charisma, persuasion, and "caring" (a smile or "attending" behavior).

The second category—Roles—includes the concepts of role complementarity, role reciprocity, treatment sector, rolecasting, and conceptual role.

Role complementarity and reciprocality are crucial elements of andragogic learning. As defined by Biddle, "roles are complementary when they fit together in that specific functions are accomplished through their joint performance" (Biddle, 78) "Roles are reciprocal when some of the characteristic behaviors of one act as sanctions for the other, and vice versa." (Biddle, 78). Since learning demands complementarity between teacher and learner roles, a "good" fit between teacher style and individual student learner style produces maximum learning. If, for instance, the teacher is authoritative and the student is self-directive, the level of complementarity is low. How much more so is this true if the majority of the students in the class are self-directive as well! Does such a teacher, incidentally, consciously or unconsciously, "prefer" to relate to those students who "seek" direction?

Role reciprocality, however, can change the learning situation. Learners, like children, can reward and/or punish their teacher. They can, for instance, shake his/her self-role congruence, especially if he/she is a beginning teacher (see Biddle, 325).

The teacher and student are a "treatment sector" (see Biddle, 325), in which the student receives "treatment" from the teacher. This "treatment" by the teacher may differ from the student's "treatment" in other "treatment sectors," such as counseling or social work education. In the latter, for instance, the student/learner has a different relationship ("treatment") with teacher and supervisor, although both treatment sectors are concerned with "educating" a social worker. This dichotomization of social work education into class and field has been a major focus of social work literature, along with the "thinker/doer" dichotomy (see, for instance, Lowy, 1968, 34; Sonnheim, 1968, 3–5; Seelig, 1991). Hamilton and Else (1983) stress that "the key to defining field work is recognizing that it is an integral part of the total curriculum of professional social work education" (13). Lowy (1978, 23, 24) seems to agree, but points out that "Field and classroom learning are two distinct modes of acquiring values, knowledge, skills and attitudes." He feels, therefore, that "classroom faculty and field instructors must be viewed as complementary teachers." (23, 24). Hokenstad and Rigby (1977), however, stress that didactic instruction "creates a situation requiring the student to be a passive recipient of knowledge in the classroom and, at the same time, an active utilizer of knowledge in the field. It thus accentuates the gap between class and field learning that the student is expected to bridge" (6).

Learning patterns in the field are defined more specifically by Berengarten and Towle (1964), while learning patterns in the classroom are compared to field learning patterns in the theory and research studies of Memmot and Brennan (1998), Kruzich, Friesen, and Van Soest (1986), (Harris, 1991), and Gross, and Hunt (cited in Urbanowski and Dwyer, 1988, 63). We will discuss these findings more fully in the section on Andragogy in Social Work Education.

In general, the treatment sector (i.e., the learning environment) is characterized by rolecasting (altercasting), defined by Biddle (63) as "Encouraging or projecting a role for the person as a part of the treatment given him or her by another." In our application, the teacher, as socializing agent, exercises interpersonal control over the student, inadvertently or "vertently" casting him/her in a role "suitable" to teacher style. In our estimation, this kind of rolecasting does not differentiate among student learning styles, and probably characterizes the pedagogue rather than the andragogue. The dilemma of the teacher is how to socialize the student into a profession while preserving and encouraging the student's unique learning style.

Both teacher and student, within the University structure, exhibit role behaviors characteristic of the context within which they interact (see Biddle,

67, 72, 229, 230). Just as pupils "become noticeably quieter when entering the door of a school building" (really?), so students entering the University classroom, "behave" in a certain "student" way! We will elaborate on this in our discussion of the Learning Center in Givat Shmuel.

The third category—Role Expectations—includes the concepts of role expectations (256, 257), expectation (119, 132), assumptions of conformity (117, 118), sanctioning (117, 118), simple formation (118), object person (122, 148)/subject person (122), expectation for self (124), and expectation for other (125).

Biddle defines role expectations as "Expectations that are structured for the roles of positions within a social system" (256). In our case, that system is the University. Students bring to this context for learning expectations from themselves and from their teachers. Biddle questions a number of assumptions about those expectations, and at least two of those assumptions are relevant for our Learning Center. The assumption of conformity, for instance, posits that roles (behaviors) are inevitably generated by role expectations. Students, for instance, "know" what the University expects from them because the 'rules" of behavior are set forth in the catalogues; therefore, they are "assumed" to conform to the rules and regulations (behavior codes). In actuality, passive learning is expected. Most "rules" are negative (student obligations), and based on grades, for instance, rather than on learning style. Students are told not only how to behave, but what to learn and, indirectly, how to pass. They are not told how to learn. Thus, an active, autonomous learner may experience difficulty in "conforming."

A further questionable assumption is that "persons conform to role expectations (solely) out of concern for sanctions." (Biddle, 117, 118). Cheating, for instance, may result in expulsion from the University. Does this threat, however, prevent cheating? Moreover, are there similar sanctions for teachers (against humiliating certain students)? Perhaps there are students and teachers who "conform" because of internalized standards! Andragogy encourages the latter, as we shall see in our discussion of the Learning Center.

Finally, congruence in student self-expectation may be congruent or incongruent with teacher self-expectation. If, for instance, a student expects him/her self to be cognitive/rational like other students, and expects his teacher to be cognitive/rational as well, he/she may be disappointed to find his teacher experiential (or pedagogic!). In such situations, the student must comply with teacher expectations out of necessity (power, authority) or out of strategy. There can, however, be a way to influence change in the teacher, especially if a group of students "contage" each other.

The fourth category—Expected Roles—includes expected role (210) and expected treatment (210). These two concepts seem to us to be the crux of teacher/learner interaction in the learning process. They are, of course, related closely to expectations. A student, for instance, "expects" certain role behaviors from a teacher, but his/her expectations that those behaviors will be exhibited may vary (from high to low) with time, during the interaction between them. Likewise, teachers expect certain role behaviors from students, and problems occur in the learning process when there is a lack of congruence between teacher and student expectations. Moreover, as Biddle points out (211), expected role may be an independent or dependent variable. Citing learning studies where teachers were "given" expectations about student learning ability, he emphasizes the effect of this "knowledge" on teacher expectations. Once again, in our estimation, the problem becomes even greater if the teacher, as a pedagogue, has an idée fixe about the class as a whole, without differentiating among individual students. And, once again, if that teacher is incapable of adjusting teaching style to individual learner style, the learning process of the class is stultified.

Expected treatment, therefore, varies with expected roles. The latter are described by Biddle as "obligations," while the former, he calls "rights." (210, 367). His definition of expected treatment: "The set of expectations for the behaviors (in context) identifies object persons that are consensually held by one or more subject persons..." (210). In the learning context of the University, the students are the "object persons" and the teachers are the "subject persons" who enunciate or hold an expectation (See Biddle, 122).

But, as we have pointed out, this is a two-way street, particularly in andragogic terms. That is, expected roles and expected treatment apply as well to students as "subject persons" and teachers as "object persons." Thus, teachers also have obligations and students also have rights. The interaction then affects the learning process.

The fifth category—System—provides the framework within which all the preceding categories occur. The two concepts in this category—Structure and Relationship—are the sine qua non without which the andragogic learning process cannot succeed.

Structure (Social), as defined by Biddle (225), is "A set of social elements that are characteristic of a given social system and are interdependent." The typical system, according to Biddle, "exhibits a characteristic (although not invariant) complement of behaviors, persons, contexts, functions, expectations, or what have you." "Classrooms," he continues, "are structured in that they typically feature a teacher, several pupils, each of whom exhibit characteristic roles." However, "the classroom roles of teacher and pupils are not independent entities; to the extent that one of these elements varies, the other is likely to vary also." Thus "structural features of the social system are not only characteristic, they are also interdependent." Roles, therefore, in his view (and ours!), "are interdependent when they are mutually facilitating or hindering of one another."

To paraphrase Biddle's example of a hospital structure, we see in the hierarchical structure of the University, a building, a means of support (i.e., administrative staff), written rules for operation, and characteristic functions in the realm of education. An intriguing footnote (267), in Biddle, suggests that our willingness to accept or resist authority stems from our relationship with our fathers. We wonder whether this has special relevance for the Israeli student in an andragogic/pedagogic learning process in social work education. The unique combination of Israeli students whose fathers fell in battle or hostile actions and their choice of social work as a profession may warrant additional study, particularly in regard to the final concept in our series—Relationship!

As we pointed out earlier, the teacher-student relationship may be compared to the "love" relationship as the interaction broadens and deepens over time. Two (or more) mutually attracted persons will come together and evolve a set of roles and activities that affords them pleasure, thus reinforcing their desires to continue the relationship (Biddle 307–310).

What, then, in andragogic terms, best characterizes the interaction between teacher and learner? What characterizes a "good" teacher, a "good" student, and the interaction between them which fosters "good" learning?

Chapter Five

Andragogy in Social Work Education

Table 5.1. "Good" Teacher/Student Interaction Characteristics

Interaction	"Good" Student	"Good" Teacher
1. Mutual Facilitation*	1. Readiness to learn (according	1. Facilitator*
2. Shared Control*	to own learning style)	2. Content Expert*
3. In and Out of Class*	2. Self-Directive	3. Resource
4. Role Expectation	3. Ability to Reflect	4. Model*
Congruence*	4. Personality Characteristics	5. Group Worker/Moderator*
5. Cue Clarity	a. Intellectual Ability	6. Socialization Agent*
6. Structural Flexibility*	b. "Sensitive"	7. Monitor of Activities*
7. Love*	c. Diligent	8. Personality Characteristics
a. Intensity	d. Ability for Critical	a. Warmth*
b. Breadth	Thinking	b. Empathy*
c. Depth	e. Openness	c. Relationship-Oriented*
	f. Enthusiasm for Subject	d. Openness*
	to be learned	e. Enthusiasm for subject*
		9. Ability to discern different
		student learning styles and plan
		accordingly*
		10. Ability to discern own
		teaching style and plan
		accordingly*
		11. Charisma*

* indicates supervisor or teacher role

Table 5.1 highlights the interaction between teacher and learner style which seem to maximize student learning. The "good" teacher, for instance, facilitates, models, and serves as a resource, while monitoring, transmitting knowledge, and serving as a socializing agent. Relationship-oriented and open, he/she possesses personality characteristics suited particularly to andragogic teaching. In addition, he/she possesses (or has "learned") an ability to identify his/her teaching style, different student learning styles, and plan accordingly.

Finally, this teacher's power to exert influence derives from charisma rather than from contextual authority alone.

The "good" student, for instance, shows a readiness to learn, albeit according to his/her own learning style, an ability to reflect (in/on), and a self-directive orientation. Personality characteristics may vary, but each characteristic or combination thereof, lend themselves to influence by the "good" teacher.

Learning, thus, proceeds from mutual facilitation, shared control, contact beyond the classroom walls, role expectation congruence, cue clarity, structural flexibility, and "love." This last concept, adapted from couple relationships, has great relevance to teacher/student relationships in andragogic terms. Biddle (307) defines "love" as "An intense mutually influencing, and mutually rewarding relationship of primary interaction between persons who are affectively bonded." If we translate the intense "love" relationship into the intense teacher/learner relationship, the three aspects of this intensity—breadth, openness, and depth—encompass a host of andragogic principles.

Breadth of a relationship (Biddle, 308) involves a wide range of characteristic behaviors. Partners spend a good deal of time together, in which they solve a majority of life's (i.e., learning) problems collectively. When love (i.e., learning) relationships are first formed, they are narrow. But those who "love" one another seek to expand the range of their shared activities, so love (i.e. learning) relationships tend to expand until they meet one or more barriers. Some of these barriers are associated with the partners. The teacher, for instance, suffers from self-role incongruence or role distance. The learner, for instance, has unrealistic (high) expectations of the teacher. Other barriers, however. may be environmental, such as inflexible role-contextualization and/or hierarchical authority structure. In general, however, the broader the relationship, the greater its potential for rewarding participants (teachers and learners) and the more difficult its management.

Openness of a relationship (Biddle, 309) involves discussion of a wide range of topics by the partners. "Love" relationships begin by being relatively closed, and tend to become more open with time. So it should be in the andragogic learning process! Unlike the case of breadth, however, most barriers to openness seem to lie within the partners. These are persons (teachers and/or students) not used to open discussions, or are threatened by them, or are unhappy in them, or who don't share broad backgrounds of agreement with their partners. So it is with teachers and learners! The andragogue reduces barriers if he/she is used to open discussion, not threatened by them, happy in the relationship, and encourages shared broad background of agreement. This type of teacher increases openness through modeling and individualizing with students with a variety of reasons for being closed (threatened, not used to openness, fear of authority figures). And, as openness increases, trust follows in its wake (see Biddle, 310) (see also, Graham, 1997; Knight, 1996, who both stress the importance of openness).

Finally, "a relationship is deep when it incorporates identities and expectations that are central to the participants" (Biddle, 310). Within a deep relationship, central identities (Biddle, 89) and expectations (Biddle, 119, 124, 125, 132, 210) are challenged, reworked and reinvested. Core aspects of the self are changed, and become committed to the relationship. The person becomes transformed and builds a new sense of his or her identity within "love." And, as Biddle comments ". . . in the final analysis, that which is evolved between the partners is a product of their interaction." (307–310).

As we shall see, relationship and interaction are crucial elements in Andragogy, Education in general, and Social Work Education in particular. In all three, breadth, openness, and depth increase during the learning process.

Nevertheless, it seems to us that social work teachers are caught on the horns of a fundamental dilemma-Are they facilitators or transmitters of knowledge? This dilemma stems from their own education for the profession. Most social work educators (see for instance Lennon, 2004, 11) are social workers first and educators second. That is, they bring to the classroom practice wisdom and some research experience/knowledge. Moreover, even as supervisors, most have taken only brief (see for instance Freeman 294–312) courses in Supervision. Very few have doctorates in Education. Thus, they probably know more about how to "help" than about how to "teach" (see, for instance, Feldman, 1972, 6). If anything, social group workers may even be better facilitators of the learning process than their casework/community organizer colleagues.

A. THE LEARNER

The learner in social work is a young adult (Lennon, 2004, 36). In the past decades, however, "mature" learners increasingly have been admitted to schools of social work, particularly at the Masters' and Doctoral levels (Marschak, 1991, 295–300). We know that adult learning demands a different approach than from child learning (although, we think andragogy is appropriate for all age groups-children as well). Learning style, therefore, varies not only according to individual but also according to age.

As mentioned earlier, Wrightsman (1994,115), discusses the dilemma of young people who want autonomy but also want "the comforting assurance that parents will always be there to help and guide" (McCrae and Costa,1990, 145 as cited in Wrightsman, 1994). They possess "condensed energy looking for a direction" but they fear that if they express their true feelings, they will not be loved.

These statements contain three concepts basic to young adult learners, which we have explored earlier in our discussion of andragogy and role theory. The young adult learner (generally between the ages of 18 and 22) wants both autonomy and direction as well as "love."

How does social work education deal with these needs (if at all!). Foeckler and Boynton (1976), in their analogy of adult learning and teaching to a railway system, state categorically that "social work education, like most American adult education, consists of a pattern of structure and expectations that is based on the experience and assumptions of elementary education." They continue, "because this idea has been extended into adult education, this process is unnecessarily rigid and highly authoritarian" (37, 38). Furthermore, "the traditional focus on information clearly predetermined the teacher's role as 'knower' and 'authority' while the role of student was that of a passive recipient of knowledge" (38).

Lowy (1978), likewise comparing andragogy and pedagogy, relates to the andragogical model. First, "an individual psychologically becomes an adult at the point at which a self'concept of essential self-direction is achieved" (3). Second, "as people mature, they accumulate an expanding reservoir of experience which become a resource for learning and at the same time provide a broadening base to which new learning can be related" (4). When that experience "is devalued or ignored, this is perceived not just as rejection of the experience, but as rejection of the adult as a person" (4). Third, time perspective between children and adults differs (4). The child's time perspective toward learning is one of postponed application, whereas adults "want to apply tomorrow what they learn today." Thus, they "enter into education with a greater problem-centered orientation to learning" (4). Fourth, Lowy then proposes a change model ("agogik") for social work practice which views social work education as a change process. The first step in this model is motivation for learning (5–7). An important part of this step is modeling. The teacher in social work education, for instance, "demonstrates by listening emphathetically to students, how they can listen empathetically to one another". (p5). Or "the teacher communicates the art of giving and receiving feedback by inviting criticism" (p6).

Lowy posits five additional steps in his model of change which include diagnosis leading to contract, selecting, implementing and evaluating the outcome of the change, and stabilizing its results. Needless to say, Lowy's approach is indeed a "road map" for the andragogic social work educactor. The problem is that, aside from rhetoric, social work educators have not translated this framework into action. And the rare research on social work education focused on learner, learning/process and learning context is spotty and not incremental (see Dalton and Kuhn, 1998; Davenport and Davenport, 1998; Kolb, 1984; Memmot and Brennan, 1998; Maypole and Day, 1998; Van Soest and Kruzich, 1994; Caspi and Reid, 2002; Johnston and Reitmeir, 1997).

We see, in summary, that a number of concepts related to the learner according to andragogy and role theory, appear in social work education. They are: learner age, autonomy/direction conflict, need for "love," activity/passivity, conflict, time perspective, relationship to authority, relationship to modeling, and change process.

B. THE LEARNING PROCESS

The learning process in social work education is similar to what we have described in our section on andragogy in higher education, but much less developed, conceptually and operationally. Loewenberg (1978) posits five general guidelines for curriculum development (10). The first, "from simple to complex content," seems to us similar to spiral or hierarchical learning. Loewenberg then presents "exemplars" for "core themes" in social work education which illustrate this guideline. Interestingly, he emphasizes that "role theory is relevant for at least five (out of seven, M.S.) of the core themes" (16)

Nor has there been any research comparison of student participation versus non student participation in the learning process in social work education, except, perhaps, for Dalton and Kuhn, 1998. (See, also, Feyrer and Whitaker, 1995, for a discussion of student empowerment models in field practicum). There has been, however, some attempt to define the rather nebulous term "student participation" in *The Handbook of Accreditation Standards and Procedures* of the CSWE (1994) and the social work literature. In the former, paragraph 5.6 (83) of *The Baccalaureate Evaluative Standards and Interpretive Guidelines* states, "consistent with the policies of the institution, the program must enable students to participate in formulating and modifying policies affecting academic and student affairs." Paragraph 6.3 (85), states that "the methods of instruction must reflect the cognitive, affective, and experiential components of learning appropriate to the attainment of the program's specified goals. Instructional methods are to involve students in their learning." What does this mean? How should the "instructor" involve students? Hokenstad and Rigby (1977) offer the andragogic answer-"a teaching strategy that engages the student." Their participation model, more prescriptive than research-based, posited a number of concepts relevant to our approach in the Givat Shmuel Learning Center. For instance, the model is appropriate for adult learners, helps social work students integrate knowledge and skill learning in a laboratory milieu, allows "occasional deviation from the chosen subject" (77), requires the "educator" to relinquish some control over the direction that the discussion takes, facilitation, and trust in oneself as a facilitator as well as trust in the student's desire to learn and evaluate him/herself. Nevertheless, the authors distinguish (78) between interaction/facilitation/participation and lack of structure. They stress that there must be a framework within which the former occur.

The literature on international social work education (*International Handbook on Social Work Education*, 1995) does not seem to reflect the participatory model. Ntusi, in an excellent paper (1995), points out that "South African social work education does not leave room for the contribution of students to the planning and presentation of the curriculum, especially at the undergraduate level" (274). Ragab, writing about social work education in the Middle East and Egypt, points out that, "decisions pertaining to degree requirements, structure, and sequencing of courses, or course contents reside with university and school administrative bodies, assisted by faculty committees. Such formal rules give students no say in the process" (297). Promotions, incidentally, depend almost solely on published work. So, we may add, why should a faculty member be a "good" teacher?

Aguilar, on the other hand, writing about social work education in Mexico and Central America, embraces Paulo Friere's "social transformation" curriculum model "to erase the traditional learning concept of knowledge flowing down to students into one in which the learners take responsibility and become the creators of their own learning process" (1995, 61). Furthermore, there should be an integration of theoretical formation and practice experience in such a way that the professional formation would "constitute a unified social theoretical process." And finally, faculty and students should "join" in a process in which "together they would search for the means to transform systems negatively impacting on the social reality of their communities" (61).

We see, then, from the articles cited, that the concept of "student participation" varies according to theoretician and may even vary according to the political philosophy of the country in which social work education occurs. Most intriguing, however, is the idea that students should experience the same process (social transformation) that they are being educated to use in their professional work in their communities (see Feldman, 1972, for an early comparison of the two processes). In casework terms, perhaps, the students experience the same "helping relationships" they are being educated to use in their professional work with individual clients. We'll expand on this later.

An additional theme stressed in education for social work is the three components of learning-cognitive, affective, and experiential. *The Handbook of Accreditation Standards and Procedures* (85) states in paragraph 6.3 that, "the methods of instruction must reflect "these" components of learning appropriate to the attainment of the program's specific goals." Hokenstad and Rigby (1977), quoting Somers' three major types of learning style (4), refer to the theorist (deductive approach to learning), the empiricist (inductive approach to learning), and the practitioner (learns by doing). And Lowy (7–8), referring to Thelen's three types of learners-the cognitive/rationale, the experiential and the experimental-suggests that "when learning groups (in social work education, M.S.) the types of learners should reflect such variation (thinking, feeling, and doing, M.S.), in order to maximize the learning potential of each person."

It seems to us that the "thinker" may be the "theorist"(cognitive/rational), the "feeler" may be the "empiricist" (affective), and the "practitioner" may be the "experimentalist" (doer/experimental). Add to this confusion, Gambrill's (1995) emphasis on the role of critical thinking in social work. According to her, "critical thinking involves the careful examination of assumptions, goals, questions, and evidence" (5). Thus, "social work should take the lead in developing models of education and practice that prepare and encourage practitioners to be critical thinkers" (p24) (See also Seelig, 1991; Meron, 1995).

But, they should also be "feelers"! That is, they must be educated to have "the freedom to feel" (Towle, 1963, 11). Just as the social work teacher faces the dilemma of transmitter/facilitator, so the student faces the dilemma of thinker/feeler. While critical thinking applies to problem-solving in both class and field, "feeling" seems secondary to "thinking" in class, and primary in field (see Towle, 1963, for an excellent discussion of the dilemma). Moreover, Feldman (1972, 6) sharpens these dilemmas when he writes "in some respects, the social work educator's role bears similarities to that of the social work practitioner" (6). He continues, "whether the developmental process is labeled education or therapy it is essentially one in which the purveyors of service directly or indirectly strive to effect change among the recipients of service and in which it is assumed the latter, as a result of active participation in the change process, will be beneficiaries of various intrinsic and extrinsic rewards that otherwise would be less available to them" (6). Thus, we may add to the teacher roles of transmitter/facilitator, the role of therapist in the change process which the student must undergo during his/her social work education.

How is the social work educator supposed to perform the tasks of his/her multiple roles? In the learning process, "every teacher must arouse the curiosity of students, provide them with a feeling that they master something that is relevant and act as a role model. Without motivation no learning takes place" (Lowy, 5). While motivation and modeling are fundamental to all learning contexts, relationship appears to receive special emphasis in social work education. It is through the relationship between teacher/therapist and student/client that motivation to change takes places.

We may carry the analogy to therapy a bit further by citing the functional model of social work built on Otto Rank's view that "the force for change had to come from within the individual, from an active, self-assertive will". "The medium through which this task is accomplished is the helping relationship" (Penn School, 1990, 6). The themes of this model are an emphasis on the participatory role of the client (read: student, M.S.) in his/her own change process, the helping relationship through which the worker (read: teacher, M.S.), came to know and understand the self (read: learning style, M.S.) presented by the client (read: student, M.S.), time phases in the development of the helping relationship. (beginning, middle, end), and the agency (read: University, M.S.) function as an organizing concept. The latter, representing society (and the social work profession, M.S.), defined function and purpose of the social worker's task (read: teacher, M.S. 7–8).

C. THE LEARNING CONTEXT

We come now to the context within which the contextual roles of teacher/ learner takes place-the University and its School of Social Work. Within these two formal structures (with sometime conflicting demands of critical thinking versus "feeling"), the learning process for professional social work unfolds. Walker (1972), writing at a time of student unrest, states that, "there is too much emphasis placed upon process rather than product on the part of the profession and the professional schools" (57). Although acknowledging that schools of social work must "practice what they preach" as "a viable instrument of liberation for oppressed people" (63), Walker states that "we must lead our students in the search for knowledge, instead of having them push us" (62). In our humble estimation, we must do both! It should be with process and product as well.

How do we do it?—We should do it through congruency between teaching and learning style. The "unmistakable identity" described by Lewis (1991, 24) may be seen in the role of performances of teacher and student, and the congruence/complementarities between them. We have already discussed at some length both teacher and student style, but we will now refer to the "principles that guide teaching" (Goldberg-Wood and Middleman 1991, 111–116). They include the principles of mutual accountability (shared control, M.S.), teaching for use, providing experience (experiential, M.S.), modeling social work ethics and values, and maximizing student to student learning (peer group influence, M.S.). Hokenstad and Rigby (1997, 5) suggest principles built on psychological theories relevant to the "teaching-learning transaction." Stimulus-response principles include positive reinforcement of learner's responses, and frequency (repetition) of that reinforcement contributes to the "incorporation of knowledge and acquisition of skills." Cognitive principles include goal setting which enhances learner motivation, provision of new ideas and experiences which can be incorporated into the learner's cognitive structure ("thinking" framework, M.S.), and encouragement of "inventive solutions" as much as of "logically correct answers" (experiential/experimental framework, M.S.). Motivation principles include differential motivation according to differential student needs, such as need for achievement ("deep learning" style, M.S.) or need for affiliation; student's cultural/sub-cultural background; group atmosphere as well as teacher learner interaction.

This last principle-group atmosphere-emphasized by Goldberg-Wood and Middleman and Hokenstad and Rigby is reinforced by Lowy, Bloksberg, and Walberg (1971, 79–80). They emphasize that student to student interaction (peer group influence) is "usually not taken into account in the teaching-learning situation."

In summary, therefore, we see that education for social work emphasizes (in theory, anyway), a facilitative learning context characterized by teacher-student-group interaction built on a number of educational principles closely resembling the andragogical approach.

D. EDUCATIONAL DILEMMAS

The andragogical approach could, in fact, resolve some of the dilemmas inherent in education for social work. We'll address five of those dilemmas in this section.

1. Generalist vs. Specialist

Watts (1995, 3), points out that "social work education, like nursing education, like teacher education is 'how' focused, or methods focused. This presents a particular challenge to social work educators, for the imparting of skills about the helping process is no easy matter."

This challenge applies, first and foremost, to the issue of the generalist vs. specialist orientation. Bernard (1995, 17), comments that "while it is clear that new areas are constantly emerging which require specialized knowledge and commitment, there is a concurrent need for more independent, autonomous practitioners with a broad service perspective. The present trend of moving from the generalist orientation (undergraduate and first year graduate education) toward specialization (second year graduate) may give way to more experimentation and different patterns. "But the teacher in this continuum is often faced with the "Academe-Practice Impasse" (Bernard, 1995, 17–20). "In order to survive in academe teachers no longer receive recognition on the basis of their practice knowledge or expertise. To remain within the academic environment, one must meet academic standards which go far beyond the capacity to teach practice skills." So much for the broad service perspective!

2. Micro vs. Macro

Within this "broad service perspective" within the generalist orientation, and within the methods focus, few teachers can fulfill all these expectation as well as those of "academe." Furthermore, few teachers have practice and theory experience in all three methods-casework, group-work, community organization.

In fact, schools of social work in the United States and other countries stress, at best, two methods only-micro/macro under a variety of names. The Council on Social Work Education Curriculum Policy Statement for Master's Degree Programs (1994), for instance, states in section m3.0 Premises Underlying Social Work Education "The purpose of social work education is to prepare competent and effective social work professionals who are committed to practice that includes services to the poor and oppressed and who work to alleviate poverty, oppression and discrimination."

In India, Mandal (1995) cites Remuchandran who "proposes that there should be two major streams of social work training-curative social work (casework, M.S.) and promotional social work (community organization, M.S.). Preferably, according to Mandal, "...training for both streams should be offered in the same institution for social work" (p362–364).

In Zimbabwe, Hampson (1995, 255), points out that although the Harare School (of Social Work, M.S.) training is presented as generic, actually there was a casework bias. Quoting a Master's thesis study, Hampson emphasizes the finding that "of respondents in the sample, only 18% overall indicated that they use all three methods in their current jobs."

Cox, writing about social work education in Asia and the Pacific (1995, 321–338), suggests that the "imported Western model" (social casework, M.S.) should be "at least" deemphasized, and suggests community and social development..."because of the mass nature of most situations of need, any focus on the individuals is unrealistic, if not also culturally and politically unacceptable." As we have mentioned already, Aguilar, writing about social work education in Mexico and Central America, unequivocally embraces Paulo Friere's social transformation curriculum model "to join faculty and students in a process in which together they would search for the means to transform systems negatively impacting on the social reality of their communities" (1995, 61).

Finally, in Israel, Guttman and Cohen (1995, 308) noted that while the BSW curriculum is built on a generalist model, there "has been a shift from social justice emphasis to clinical practice and mental health," and "indeed, the pressure for greater clinical content seems to come largely from students and from the field," although "many of the faculty would prefer a stronger emphasis on the social justice aspects of social work."

Once again, we encounter the question of who leads whom as well as the influence of the political/cultural environment within which social work education occurs. Group work, incidentally, seems lost somewhere between the other two methods of social work practice (see, for instance, Birnbaum and Auerbach, 1994). We may add, semantically speaking, animals may be trained, but students should be educated! (see, also, Hewitt, 1995, 162–163).

3. Simple vs. Complex

Three of Loewenberg's five general guidelines for curriculum development relate to this issue. Learning should proceed from simple to complex content, from familiar to unfamiliar content, and from proximate to more distant content (1978, p10) (see also Lowy, 1978, 24). Theoretically, these guidelines may be compared to the cognitive learning steps of Gagne (Lowry, 1978, 17) the spiral learning of the McMaster model (Neufeld and Barrows, 1984) and the integrative "threading" model described by Lowy (1978, p9).

In field instruction, as well, Wilson (1981, Chapter 7) suggests selecting appropriate learning experiences for the student, including moving from the simple to the complex, and providing mastery of a "small arena" which gives the student confidence to apply skills to a broader horizon (89).

Unfortunately, none of the general guidelines or "small arenas" have been defined operationally and tested systematically. What is "simple"? What is "complex"? What is "in-between"? What is "familiar" and "unfamiliar"? What is "proximate" and "distant"? What is hierarchical and what is spiral? Do the guidelines apply equally to each method? That is, simple to complex in casework, group-work, community/organization? Or, should they cut across methods? That is, learning role theory, for instance, in relation to the individual, the group, and the community rather than separately *within* each method. (see Bourke, 1987; Tourse, R.W.C., McInnis-Dittrich, and Platt, S., 1999).

"Training" for "competence" *does not* answer these questions. Nor does curriculum built on the "practice wisdom" of social work education clarify the issue. In essence, that education is built on courses with some logical relationships horizontally and vertically to each other and to field work, but with a coterie of teachers and supervisors generally "academically free" to teach and supervise with some latitude.

4. Class vs. Field

There *appears* to be consensus in the social work literature that "the key to defining field education is recognizing that it is an integral part of the total curriculum of professional social work education" (Hamilton and Else, 1983, p13). But almost in the same breath, "field and classroom learning are two distinct modes of acquiring values, knowledge, skills and attitudes" (Lowy, 1978, p23). The "total educational program is comprised of two related yet distinctive parts: the theory-oriented academic content of the curriculum and the case-oriented learning which takes place in the practicum" (Bourke, 1987, p6). The latter is termed by Lowy (1978, 23), the confrontation with the real world in which "the principles of continuity, progression, and integration, "provide" repeated opportunities for thinking, feeling, and doing related to each curriculum element." (Hamilton and Else, 1983, 14–17).

5. Education vs. Therapy

How do the teachers in those two "worlds"-the "academic" and the "real" resemble or differ from each other? Or why should they differ? Here, too, the literature confuses us. Charlotte Towle (1963, 1) defines supervision as "a process in the conduct of which the supervisor has three functions-administration, teaching, and helping. Her mid-position has significance in the performance of each of these functions, and notably in "helping." She stresses that "a teaching situation differs from a psychological therapeutic session, a class from a therapy group session, in its heavy reliance upon the student's capacity to experience change in feeling and thereby change in thinking through an intellectual approach." Towle, however, cannot free herself from the use of such therapeutic language as "unresolved authority-dependency conflicts, intimacy-versus-isolation conflicts, attachments to the past, and over identification." While these terms as we too have pointed out, identify the young adult learner, classroom teachers seem to leave the "feeling" change focus to the field supervisor/instructor! The field teacher uses the "helping relationship" to enable the student learner to "resolve" these conflicts. As Berengarten and Towle point out (1964), there are aggressive and passive learners (Towle's definitions) or experiential-empathetic, intellectual-empathetic, and doers (Berengarten's definition) who require differential educational diagnoses and supervisory interventions.

Sowers-Hoag and Thyer (1985), in their review of empirical research on teaching social work practice, also find heavy focus on such "core facilitative clinical skills" as communicating empathy, non-possessive warmth, and genuineness. In fact, performance was enhanced on ten skills better in laboratory experience rather than in didactic instruction.

Nevertheless, while Lowy (1978, p23–24) sees classroom faculty and field instructors as "complementary teachers," "we still know woefully little about the reciprocal effects of these two modes of experiences and how their complementarity can be enhanced" (26).

Meanwhile, Cloward (1998, 584–586) decries the "divorce between professional education and professional practice." "In many schools of social work, rich professional experience and superior practice teaching competence now have little, even no, weight in winning promotion and tenure." In his estimation, classroom teaching is becoming more about learning to conduct research on practice than about learning practice itself.

We see, then, that classroom teacher role performance may differ from field teacher role performance, and that the former may focus more on knowledge transmission than on "feeling" transmission. The latter, moreover, may focus more on personality change via therapeutic interventions rather than on knowledge change. Both encourage a change process, and both attempt to facilitate. But where is the systematic complementarity and why can't all functions reside within the same teacher? This will be addressed further in the section on the Givat Shmuel Learning Center.

E. THE "BRIDGE"

In social work education, the putative bridge connecting learner, learning process and learning context is the field experience. It embodies all five dilemmas-generalist/specialist, micro/macro, simple/complex, class/field, and education/therapy. It both parallels and complements classroom teaching dilemmas. Its form is more varied and more complex than classroom structure. Field work models run the gamut from highly structured field units or faculty-led training centers where the University maintains major control of student education to individualized models which are less structured and rely ultimately on faculty field liaison and field instructor relationship to ensure that the educational goals of the University are being met through appropriate learning and teaching processes (Bogo and Globerman, 1995). Field instruction supervision-teaching may be individual, dyadic, or group. The latter is viewed "as one way to accommodate the reduction of agency time allocated for field education" (Bogo, Globerman, and Sussman, 2004). This seems to us the right idea but for the wrong reason! Bogo et al., add that group supervision "provides the opportunity to learn from others through sharing knowledge, hearing different perspectives, and discussing issues both common and unique to each group member."

Unfortunately, however, "only one-third of MSW students are likely to graduate with any experience in working with groups" (Birnbaum and Auerbach, 1994, 332). According to Birnbaum and Auerbach, "field instructors lack the necessary training to provide group practice supervision." According to Glassman (1995, 185–192), "field instructors need help in teaching foundation practice skills and teaching social work methods...as a result of the generic curriculum of the last two decades, fewer people know about group work and community organization" (see, also, Szewello and Shragge, 1995). Even more critical than field instructor weakness in group work and community organization, is the fact that field instructors lack the formal teaching experience that is instrumental in being a field instructor (see Freeman and Hansen, 1995). Finally, field instructors are underpaid (see Lennon, 2004) and undervalued (Lager and Robbins, 2004, 8; Bogo, Globerman, and Sussman, 2004).

That, "bridge," therefore, is very shaky and its promise largely unfulfilled. As Caspi and Reid (2002) point out, "the literature on supervision is both vast and disconnected." "It includes many 'expert' suggestions and a body of empirically supported recommendations to guide a broad spectrum of supervisory considerations" (174).

Take heart, for field instructors are not alone in their "deficiencies." Classroom teachers, too, lack adequate preparation for their teaching functions! Though better paid and valued than field teachers (Lennon, 2004), the "sad truth, according to some authorities, is that most teachers are uninspired people who simply work for a living and have no wish to be stimulated to greater investment of time, energy, or spirit...They assign basic books and then summarize them for students" (Bell, 1972, 47–48). Citing Cahn (1978), Wooldridge (1995) states, "it is a sad but indisputable fact that much of the teaching that goes on in our colleges and universities is of very poor quality . . . Intellectual competence and pedagogical (there is that 'wrong' word, again! M.S.) competence are two very different qualities."

According to Wooldridge, "traditional doctoral programs, which form the core of the training of university faculty, do not concern themselves with teaching future faculty about the teaching and learning process." Valentine, et al. (1998) reporting on a national survey of 51 social work doctoral program directors, support Wooldridge's conclusions ". . . although the majority of doctoral programs include preparation for teaching as a program objective, they offer limited formal course work and few opportunities for supervised teaching experiences" (273). Moreover, "the results reflect the perspective that preparing educators is not viewed as the primary mission of social work doctoral programs, and that if a choice must be made between preparing researchers or educators, doctoral programs prefer the former" (279).

Therefore, education for social work is built on at least three fallacious assumptions:

1. Conducting research in a field qualifies one to teach.
2. Practice in a field qualifies one to supervise.
3. The researcher-teacher and the practice-teacher complement each other.

What, then, if anything, can be said positively about class and field teachers, their similarities and dissimilarities, and their unique contributions to education for social work? We will try to answer these questions in three ways. First, we will attempt to apply the framework of the three theories we have described-role theory, learning theory, and andragogy. Second, we will use these theories in regard to the learner, the learning process and the learning context. Third, we will focus on selected teaching functions which do indeed distinguish between class and field. Finally, we will interpret the results of our field study within the perspective of the overall framework.

A. THREE THEORY FRAMEWORK

1. Role Theory

A second look at Tables 4.3 and 4.4 indicates that class and field teachers are more similar than dissimilar in their tasks and role behaviors. Role theory, provides us with a "road map" for educating, selecting and monitoring social work faculty (class and field).

The facilitation role is mentioned most frequently in the literature on classroom teachers and field instructors. At least three roles differentiate between class and field teacher both in type and in essence.

Gatekeeper- (Hartman and Wills 310–319) The term itself is an euphemistic way of saying 'pass' or 'fail'-the 'gateway' to the profession. This power vested in the class and field teacher has its limits (Lager and Robbins

2004, 6). The classroom teacher can more easily fail the student on objective criteria—papers and exams—than on the basis of personality characteristics, such as insensitivity to client needs or lack of acceptance of client difference. These characteristics may appear in classroom discussions or term papers, but may be more difficult to prove than lack of intellectual ability or critical thinking to an Appeals Committee.

The field teacher, involved in a quasi-therapeutic relationship with the student (Knight, 1996 p400), in the "real world" can perhaps, more easily fail the student on the basis of personality characteristics, albeit subjective, or on the more "objective" criterion of causing "damage" to the client. In addition, lack of intellectual ability, critical thinking and inability to apply theory to practice, i.e. complementarity between class and field teacher, may, indeed, "close the gate" to such a student. Lager and Robbins (2004), however, point out "enormous constraints" on the gate-keeper role in public universities and on the part of students themselves who "pay for the product" to which they are entitled regardless of how their performance is evaluated" (p6).

What happens, when the "thinker" receives high grades in course work but does poorly as a "doer"? (see Coleman, Collins and Atkins, 1995, 253,266) The emphasis of academe on intellectual success combined with the under-valued position of field work (and its grade) make gatekeeping more difficult. At any rate, the success rate of gatekeeping may be very low (see Gibbs and Blakely, 2000, for a comprehensive review of gatekeeping).

Both the classroom teacher and the "quasi-therapeutic" field teacher seem reluctant to "close the gate" too readily. They are willing to invest time and energy in developing "problematic" students, and perhaps rightfully so, for we are, first and foremost, social workers.

See, therefore, for instance three very interesting descriptive articles dealing with learner types. The first, by Urania Glassman (1995, 185–192) suggests a process model to "help field instructors to be more effective teachers" with nine types of student learners-the non-affective thinker, the feeler, the doer, the fraidy cat, the I-Am-Not-A Student, the Me, I-Am-Only-A-Student, the Starkly Different, the Know-It-All, and the I Don't Trust Authority. The second article, by Thomlinson and Collins (1995, 223–228) describes a structured consultation workshop for field supervisors illustrating "three types of student learning situations" utilizing role play in order to help the supervisors to help: the Marginal or Failing Student, the Bright but Compliant Student, and the Student who Avoids Change and Progress. The authors relate to the gatekeeper role, commenting that "it may at times be difficult...to assess a student as unsatisfactory because of the student's reaction, as well as the reactions of the field liaison and field coordinator."

The third article, by Salmon, Getzel and Kurland (1991, 65–80), like the first article, does not deal specifically with supervision or gate-keeping, but does deal with learner types. The focus is on group work students, although the authors state that "these principles and techniques also are relevant for teaching other social work practice methods." The authors then describe four types of students-The Neophyte, the Thinker, the Natural, and the Star-and "some of the ways instructors can approach their work so that increased skill and increased knowledge can be the result for most of their students."

2. Model

The next most frequently mentioned role for both class and field teacher is that of model (often mentioned along with facilitator role in the same article) (Caspi and Reid, 2002, 139; Rainey and Kolb, 1995, 136; Salmon, Getzel, Kurland, 1991, 68, 69; Knight, 2001, 508, 512–516, 519–520; Lewis, 1991, 20, 24; Graham, 1997; Rogers, 1996; Knight, 1996, 400–401). What better way for them to facilitate learning the social work profession than by modeling professional behavior! But what does this mean? Kramer and Wrenn, for instance, adapting from Knowles' Andragogical Table (1978), present the principle that "the teacher accepts each student as a person of worth and respects his/her feelings and ideas" (59). They present the implementation techniques of this principle as "model good communication skills, appreciation and respect for student's verbal contributions in class, and encourage students to do so" (51). "Ask students about their areas of knowledge and interest early in class and refer to these throughout the course" (51). Knight, in her study of the skills of teaching social work practice, concludes that ("in data based solely on the perceptions of students") "the results suggest that it is important for the instructor to serve as a model of a social work professional." Rainey and Kolb see the teacher as a role model and colleague in an "affectively oriented" learning environment. Lewis (1999, 20) stressing "the use of professional self as teacher in helping students to learn," points out that he himself would have to model "risk-taking" behavior by his own participation in class and conferences in order to teach his students to risk uncertainty "in order to know more and differently." He, in what I, (M.S.) as a Penn School graduate see as the Functional Approach, stresses using himself in a self-conscious, self-critical way to model what he wants from his students. Finally, Knight, in her study of field instructors, stresses the supervisor's "quasi-therapeutic" function and as a role model in which the emphasis is on "learning through doing." In group work, for instance, according to Salmon, Getzel and Kurland, "the teacher needs to be extremely active with the Neophyte," role modeling so that "the student will see and learn, in action, the manner in which the 'master' moves to operationalization and generalization through comments made on written assignments, through individual conferences with the student, and through teaching in the classroom" (1991, 68, 69)

3. "Love" Partner

Erotic connotations aside, this role can be a particularly powerful one in the learning process. Setting aside andragogic principles for a moment, and using Biddle's definition of "love," let's examine this role in terms of the social work literature. Both class and field teachers can be "love" partners, but they differ on the three aspects of that "intense relationship."

The classroom teacher, generally does not spend a "good deal of time together" with the students in his/her class. Barriers such as role distancing on the part of the teacher or unrealistic student expectations of him/her as the hierarchical authority structure tend to limit the breadth of the relationship.

The classroom teacher, however, does have the opportunity to spend time together with the students, to expand the range of their shared activities, to solve problems collectively, and to soften the barrier of hierarchical authority. Potter and East (2000, p228, 230, 233), reporting on an MSW Integrative Field Seminar, utilizing Reflective Judgment stress a developmental, process oriented context. The class was small (10–12 students), and was a "year long experience in which the same group of thinkers work together with focus on the integration of classroom and fieldwork learning" (230). They suggest, like Lewis, that effective teachers, "are comfortable with ambiguity" (228). They suggest that effective teachers "join with students and enjoy the developmental journey" (228). Additionally, "they (the students) must engage with "us" (the teachers), both in and out of the classroom in tasks which require high levels of reflective thinking so that they experience critical thinking at the heart of the social work profession" (233).

Unfortunately, "their" (the teacher's) "primary sin is their arrogance in assuming that they are there solely to teach and to correct and students are there solely to learn and to admire" (Bell, 1972, 46). It seems that in terms of breadth of relationship, the classroom teacher may not be a very effective "love" partner.

The classroom teacher fares not much better in the openness of the relationship with his/her students. The literature criticizes more than praises in this area as well. Graham (1997, 34, 43) traces the history of that criticism of teachers in general and of social work teachers, in particular. Dewey "criticized traditional teaching methods as "telling," Bruner used the term, "passionless classroom," Freire decried the lack of "student empowerment," and Graham herself criticized the lack of "stretch" (flexibility!, M.S.) in faculty members' ability to "stay abreast of changing student needs." Finally, she cites Mercado, who stresses the "centrality of caring"-being there, being real, being open, and being fair."

O'Neal (1996, 143), citing Davis (185–186), also stresses that "establishing a classroom that encourages thinking" requires, among other points, "encouraging open discussion" and "appreciating individuality and openness." It seems that without openness, barriers cannot be reduced, trust follows not in its wake, and learning cannot reach its optimal level.

How, then, can the depth of the relationship produce a change in the "core aspects of the self" and a "new sense of identity" (i.e. a professional social worker). If, as we pointed out earlier in our discussion of role theory, mutual expectations are unfulfilled, both teacher and student are disappointed in the 'love" relationship and learning-true learning-does not take place. But does even "quasi-therapy" occur? That, too, can produce a change in self-identity, and thus, in learning. Must the teacher "mirror the helping process" he/she endeavors to teach the students? Graham (1997, 35) thinks "yes." Shulman (1987, 3) seems to think "no." "It is important for educators to integrate content and process without making the class into a therapy group."

Theoretically, the field teacher, can indeed provide "quasi-therapy" (whatever that is, conceptually and operationally) in his/her love partner relationship with the student learner. Theoretically, that same field teacher has certain advantages over the class teacher in breadth, openness and depth of the relationship. First, the relationship is one-to-one or, at most, one-to-small group. Second, the field teacher, by virtue of learning group size and length of time together, can invest more in the quasi-therapeutic learning process. That is, classroom learning, except, perhaps, for methods courses, is semester length and "large" group (25 or more students) (see CSWE, 1994, McMurty and McClelland, 1997). Third, both emotional and environmental barriers can, perhaps, be more successfully overcome through a combination of the above during the supervisory process. The student/learner thus, hopefully, experiences a personal and a professional transformation.

The literature, more hortatory than research, provides partial support for these assumptions. Knight (1996), for instance, cited studies that found that supervisors who were described by their students as available to them were seen as "helpful," and she, herself found that "the field instructor's availability outside of the regularly scheduled supervisory time was a consistent predictor of favorable student assessments" (411). In a later study, however, Knight (2001, 375, 377) found that while field instruction is a "process," amount of supervisory time and the supervision decreased as the field practicum progressed. She speculated that this may reflect increased confidence in students' abilities or increasing demands on the instructor's time (375).

Although both studies have their limitations (1996, 402,404; 2001. 373–375), time together and stage of process appear to be important factors in the learning relationship.

"Openness" also is an important factor in the field teacher-student learning relationship. Citing Lemberger and Marshack, Freeman and Hansen, (1995, 300) note that "the ideal model of field instruction is one of mutuality, a model that intimates that both parties are honest, mature, and open to learning." Knight (1996), also found that students "rated as more helpful field instructors who encouraged them to develop their own style and who fostered open discussion" (1996, 400). (See, also, Raphael and Rosenblum, 1991).

Finally, the "deep" relationship between field teacher and student developed during the course of the year, in a quasi-therapeutic way, should indeed challenge, rework, and reinvest core aspects of the self. Thus, the student becomes "transformed" emotionally and, hopefully, intellectually into a "professional social worker."

4. Learning Theory

Learning theory, like role theory, increases our understanding of the three-way interaction among class teacher, field teacher, and student. A number of research studies and at least "32 commercially published instruments are used by researchers and educators to assess the different dimensions of learning style" (Campbell, 1991, cited in Sims and Sims, 1995, 194). According to Kolb and Dunn and Dunn, there are at least 18 different student learning styles (cited in Sternberg, 1997) and at least six teacher styles (Henson and Borthwick, cited in Sternberg, 1997). In the literature we surveyed, we found 52 types of student learning, 16 of which appeared to characterize both class and field learning, 18 seemed to be unique to class learning, and 18 seemed unique to field learning, as shown in table 5.2.

From that list, we will focus on a number of types which seem best to characterize social workers in general and social work students in particular. Three important books (Kolb, 1984; Sims and Sims 1995; Sternberg, 1997) and several studies (Walz and Uematsu, 1993; Van Soest and Kruzich, 1994; Rainey and Kolb, 1995; and Raschick, Maypole and Day, 1998) provide us with conceptual and operational definitions and statistics concerning the following types.

a. Accommodator-Combines active experimentation and concrete experience, and tends to be people-oriented and learns through trial-and-error problem solving. (Characterizes student in field).

Table 5.2.   Social Work Student Learning Types

	Class	Field
Surface	X	X
Deep	X	X
Serialist	X	X
Holist	X	X
Level 1	X	
Level 2		X
Level 3		X
Theorist	X	
Empiricist		X
Practitioner (Doing)		X
Cognitive/Rational	X	
Experiential		X
Experimental	X	X
Experiential/Empathetic		X
Intellectual/Empathetic	X	
Doer		X
Accommodator		X
Diverger		X
Assimilator	X	
Converger	X	
Cognitive	X(more in class than in field)	X
Structure	X	X
Sharer	X	X
Competitive	X	X
Turned-Off	X	
Executive	X	
Legislative	X	X
Judicial	X	
Monarchic	X	X
Hierarchic	X	
Oligarchic		X
Anarchic		X
Liberal		X

Conservative	X	
Left Brain	X (70%)	
Right Brain		X (30 %)
Field Dependent		X
Field Independent	X	X
Dependent	X	
Collaborative		X
Independent		X
Thinking	X	
Feeling		X
External	X	X
Internal	X	
Concrete Experience (CE)		X
Reflective Observation (RO)	X	X
Reflective in Action (RI)		X
Abstract Conceptualization (AC)	X	
Abstract Experimentation (AE)		X
Local	X	X
Global	X	X

b. Assimilator-Combines reflective observation and abstract conceptual-
    ization. Characterized by abstract thinking and theoretical orientation.
    (Characterizes student in class).
c. Diverger-Combines concrete experience and reflective observation.
    Tends to use information from their senses and feelings (Characterizes
    student in field).
d. Converger-Combines abstract conceptualization and active experimenta-
    tion. Tends to have a good understanding of practical ideas and theoreti-
    cal application (Characterizes student in class).
e. Executive-Likes to follow rules and prefers problems that are pre-struc-
    tured or prefabricated. Does what he/she is told. (Characterizes student in
    class. Probably resembles Converger).
f. Legislative-Likes to come up with his/her own way of doing things and
    prefers to decide for him/herself what he/she will do, and how to do it.
    Likes to make own rules and prefers problems that are not pre-structured

or pre-fabricated. This is conducive to creativity (Characterizes student in field. Probably resembles Diverger).

g. Judicial-Likes to evaluate rules and procedures, and prefers problems in which one analyzes and evaluates existing things and ideas. (Characterizes student in class. Probably resembles Converger).

h. Monarchic-Single-minded and driven. Can be counted on to get things done (Characterizes student more in field than in class. Probably resembles doer).

i. Hierarchic-Has a hierarchy of goals and recognizes the need to set priorities. More accepting than Monarchic of complexity. (Characterizes student more in field than in class. Probably resembles doer).

j. Oligarchic-Like the Hierarchic in desire to do more than one thing within the same time frame, but unlike the hierarchic, tends to be motivated by several, often competing goals of equal perceived importance. Pressured by competing demands and not always sure what to do first. (Characterizes student in field).

k. Anarachic-seems motivated by potpourri of needs and goals that can be difficult for person, as well as for others, to sort out. Seems to take a random approach to problems. Rejects rigid rules (Characterizes student in field).

l. Liberal-Likes to go beyond existing rules and procedures to maximize change and seek situations that are somewhat ambiguous. "Trouble-seeker" and becomes bored easily (Characterizes student in field).

m. Conservative-Likes to adhere to existing rules and procedures, minimize change, avoid ambiguous situations in work and professional life. Happiest in structured and relatively predictable environment (Characterizes student more in class than in field).

n. Left-Brain Dominant-Does lineal, rational, sequential types of processing. 70 percent of people are left-brained. Wants simple answers to complex questions. (Characterizes student in class. Probably resembles thinker). Unemotional, logical and rational in working with crises.

o. Right-Brain Dominant-Uses a global process in which data is perceived, absorbed, and processed even while it is in the process of changing. 30 percent of people are right-brained. Less organized than Left-brained, but better than them in interpersonal relations and people motivation. Don't follow through with details, and uses emotions instead of logic. (Characterizes student in field. Probably resembles Doer).

p. Field Dependent-Learning is a social experience (Characterizes student in field).

q. Field Independent-Prefers formal learning. More reflective and analytical than field dependent person. (Characterizes student probably more in class).
r. Reflection on Action- Reflects on his/her actions after an event. "In order to explore experiences in order to lead to new understandings and appreciations". (May characterize student both in class and field, though more likely in class).
s. Reflections in Action-Reflections which occurs in the midst of experience "in order to lead to new understandings and appreciation." (Characterizes student primarily in field).

Now we can present a profile of the characteristics of the student "most appropriate" for classroom learning (the "good" class student) and most appropriate for field learning

a. Classroom student—Left-brain dominant, (unemotional, logical and rational), field independent. He is an Assimilator-Converger who prefers pre-structured problems, avoids ambiguous situations where possible, follows rules, analyzes and evaluates ideas presented in class, recognizes the need to set priorities, and learns by reflecting on his actions (i.e. problem solving in class). He is the thinker-rational, sequential, and analytic.
b. Field Student-Right-brain dominant, field dependent, she is an Accommodator-Diverger who prefers problems that are not pre-structured or prefabricated, requiring creativity in their solution. She is single-minded, and can be counted on to get things done. She is, however, not always sure what to do first, seems to take a random approach to problems (in spite of her single-mindedness) and seems motivated by a potpourri of needs and goals that can be difficult for her as well as for others. She rejects rigid rules, seeks situations that are somewhat ambiguous, and likes to maximize change. She learns primarily by reflecting on her actions while still in the midst of them. She is the doer-emotional, random (non-sequential), and creative.

With these profiles in hand, the respective teachers-class and field-should recognize the type of student they are receiving, plan accordingly the learning process most appropriate for each student's "transformation" into a professional social worker, and adapt their own teaching style to individual student needs. A number of problems, however, make the process quite complicated.

First, the profile for classroom learning may be less appropriate for field learning. An unemotional, logical, and rational student, for instance, may be able to analyze his client's problems, but not relate emotionally. On the other hand, the profile for field learning may be less appropriate for classroom learning. She may relate emotionally to her clients, but may experience difficulty in setting intervention (problem solving) priorities. Brain dominance is thus but one example of "characteristic cognitive, affective and physiological behaviors that serve as relatively stable indicators of how learners perceive, interact with, and respond to the learning environment" (Sims and Sims, 1995 XII).

A number of studies of social work students and social workers using the Kolb Learning Style Inventory (LSI) found consistently that graduate students were Divergers, undergraduate students "most likely to be Accommodators" (Reviewed in Van Soest and Kruzich); social workers were Accommodators (Miller and Kennedy, 1979; Middleman and Rhodes, 1985, as cited in Van Soest and Kruzich). Divergers and Accommodators (Kolb, 1984). In addition, Raschick, Maypole and Day (1998) found that field students were Accommodators, "who by definition deemphasize abstract and reflective learning," outnumbering those in the other learning quadrants of Kolb's conceptual model.

We see, then, that these "preferred learning styles" of social workers are consistent study to study. Are they, however, amenable to change? This is our second issue. Sims and Sims, citing Kimble and Garmezy, 1963 (Sims and Sims 1995, 2) define learning as "a relatively permanent change in an attitude or behavior that occurs as a result of repeated experience." This means that the "relatively stable indicators of how learners respond to the learning environment" can indeed be "transformed." A new set of "stable indicators" occurs. Thus, in the case of brain hemisphericity (brain dominance), "Experiments have shown that stimulation and encouragement of cooperation between weaker and stronger side can bring great increase in ability and effectiveness" (Sims and Sims, 1995, 9–10). In social work, therefore, the same student can be analytic and unemotional in class and analytic and emotional in the field. Moreover, learning style or preference can change with status, age, and/or gender. Kolb (1984) found, for instance, that for career advancement in social work (from direct service to administration) "the basic Accommodator style begins to require a backup of Converger skills or perhaps even Assimilator (social planning) skills (185). Compared to engineering alumni, however, social work alumni show much more variation in learning style and their careers are "primarily of a dual-track nature" (185). That is, in engineering "there is a definite general progression from direct engineering work to managerial positions . . .,whereas social work appears to have two tracks, administrative and direct service; that begin in graduate school and continue equally in early and late career with less distinct progression from one role to the next," (185).

As for age and gender, Van Soest and Kruzich (1994) found that there were no significant differences in learning style "between students who are younger and older than the median age for each group," nor did male and female students "vary significantly in preferred learning styles" (58). "Feminist pedagogy," which we will discuss shortly, may, however, produce research which will show gender differences in learning style. Not by chance did we profile a classroom student as male and a field student as female!

Learning environment probably also interacts with learning style. That is, the "relatively stable" learning preference of a student may change (or, perhaps, adapt temporarily) to the environment in which the student is expected to learn. In social work education, for instance, the student "learns" both in the academic setting of the University and in the real world setting of a social agency. The literature tells us that there are differences in the expectations of these two settings. Lager and Robbins, citing Rhodes, Ward, Ligon and Priddy (1999) (in Lager and Robbins, 2004, 7), list "seven current threats to field education," four of which seem to differentiate the two environments- "the academization of schools of social work, the loss of autonomy in the larger academic systems, the devaluation of field directors, and a lack of faculty commitment to field education." Moreover, a fifth threat-erosion of the gatekeeping role of field instructors-suggests that while public universities influence their schools of social work to accommodate more students with serious psychological and social problems, field teachers experience "enormous constraints in their effort to weed troubled students out of the program . . . thus preventing them from entering the profession. Why? Because these students frequently are able to complete the academic prerequisites of field satisfactorily" (7).

As we have seen, however, from Kolb's comparison of professional education in social work and engineering (1984), social work students are not alone in their need to adapt to different learning environments. Those environments, moreover, are more complex than the simple dichotomy between class (university) and field (agency). Discussing Fry's concept of the learning environment (Fry, 1978, 197 in Kolb, 1984), Kolb describes the four "pure" types of learning environment:

1. Affectively complex-Emphasis on experiencing what it is actually like to be a professional in the field under study. Expressions of feelings, "are encouraged and seen as productive inputs to the learning process." We see this type as characteristic of field agency learning.

2. Perceptually complex-Primary goal is understanding something: "to be able to identify relationships between concepts, to be able to define problems for investigation, to be able to collect relevant information, to be able to research a question. . . ." We see this type as characteristic of classroom learning.
3. Symbolically complex-Learner "is involved in solving a problem for which there is usually a right answer or a best solution." Information source is abstract and there are "rules of inference." We see this type as also characteristic of classroom learning.
4. Behaviorally complex-Emphasis is upon "actively applying knowledge or skills to a practical problem which need not have a right or best answer. . . . this would normally be a 'real life' problem and the focus is on doing." We see this type as characteristic of field agency learning.

Nevertheless, as Kolb points out, "learning environments vary in the degree to which they are oriented to any of the four pure types." Thus, Fry (1978) cited in Kolb (1984, 197–200) showed in a study of a large architecture department. This may also occur in schools of social work-perceptual and symbolic in the classroom/university setting as well as in the field agency setting or affective and behavioral in field agency setting as well as in the classroom (laboratory?/University setting).

The field work agency in social work education complicates the picture even more. As Bisno and Cox point out, "In practice, social workers may concentrate on social arrangements or on the interior life of individuals, rather on the nexus of the two." (Bisno and Cox, 1997, 374). It seems to us that students placed in these types of agencies may experience different types of learning environments-the former (social welfare offices) demanding competency in making social arrangements (behaviorally complex); the latter (family service or mental health agency) demanding competency in theories governing family relationships or psychiatric problems. Obviously, here, too, the type lines are blurred.

But learning environment, like learning style, can be changed. Unfortunately, however, "when students arrive in professional school heavily indoctrinated by years of passive ingestion and superficial conformity and when advising procedures and field work experiences in those schools reinforce dependence and conformity; it may be and often is difficult to convince them that free and adventuresome involvement is actually the classroom goal." "It is also incredibly difficult to sustain such an ethos when universities rely so heavily on required courses, objective examinations, and grading systems" (Bell, 1972, 47). "The student soon learns that he is at college to be processed." His goal often becomes how to get through rather than learning in itself". (Swanson, 1972, 78). Written more than three decades ago, by a professor of social work and a student of social work respectively, these criticisms of the university as a "large bureaucratic system to which the individual must adapt and not the system to the individual" (Swanson, 1972, 77), seem just as relevant and fresh today.

Who, then, can change that system and how?

The teacher, (class and field), the individual student, and the group of other students with whom they interact! Disappointingly, however, there is little research on teacher style, and even less on the interaction between teacher style and learner style, and almost nothing on teacher/multiple student interaction in the learning environment.

As far as teacher style is concerned, there is no instrument, such as TSI (Teacher Style Inventory) comparable to LSI (Learning Style Inventory). However, Sternberg (1997) has developed and used a Thinking Style Questionnaire for Teachers (which may or may not correspond to the teacher's own preferred learning style or styles) and tested it in a private and public school. He found that older teachers were more executive, local and conservative than younger teachers. Kolb's Learning Style Inventory (LSI), "the most widely used assessment instrument for examining learning styles" (Van Soest and Kruzich, 1994, 65) is considered appropriate as a descriptive tool, "even by those who are critical of the instrument" (See, for instance, a comparison of the Kolb and Jarvis Models in Miller, Kovacs, Wright, Corcoran, and Rosenblum, 2005 which stress "the role of reflection, relationship, and context in understanding adult learning" 144). Thus, researchers, using the instrument, have found that the class situation favors Convergers, while the field practice and the field favors Divergers (Memmot and Brennan, 1998, 75–98); Kruzich, Friesen and Van Soest (1986, 22–30); More specifically, "faculty teaching micro-practice were most often Convergers while faculty teaching macro-practice were primarily Assimilators." "In contrast, a majority of graduate students and field instructors were Divergers, with the undergraduate students most likely to be Accommodators." (Kruzich, Friesen and Van Soest, 1986, cited in Van Soest and Kruzich).

The evidence seems significantly consistent to allow us now to present a profile of the characteristics of the class and field teacher.

1. Classroom Teacher-Left brain dominant Assimilator-Converger, likes to follow rules, prefers problems that are pre-structured, and tries to avoid ambiguous situations where possible. Recognizes the need to set priorities through reflective observation and abstract conceptualization. He is the Thinker-rational, sequential, and analytic.

2. Field Teacher-Right-brain dominant, field dependent, she is an Accommodator Converger, who prefers problems requiring creativity in their solution. Although not always sure what to do first, she can handle ambiguous
situations, and emphasize concrete experience. She is the Doer, emotional,
random (non-sequential), and creative.

Our four, stereotypical, profiles-classroom student, field student, class
teacher, and field teacher, theoretically, should provide us with an interaction
pattern most conducive to maximum learning. The "ideal" class learning environment, should match the left-brain dominant, Assimilator-Diverger student
with his classroom teacher counterpart. The literature, however, tells us otherwise. There can be match, partial match, mismatch, change over time. Kolb
(1984, 182) suggests that "rather than being a cause of successful academic
performance, motivation to learn may well be a result of learning climates that
match learning styles and thereby produce successful learning experiences."
Citing Fry, 1978 and Kolb, 1976, he emphasized the importance of faculty
tailoring their teaching to the individual student learning styles described in
his theory (200, 201). Lewis (1991), on the other hand, emphasized that "a
student's efforts to mimic her teacher's style and the teacher's encouragement
of students to enrich their individual styles both suggest assumptions about
the nature and origin of styles that deserve more attention" (24). But Lewis
views his own style as "relatively stable" (28). While Lewis' statements are
more philosophical, Kolb's statements are research-based.

A number of other studies showed that:

1. Students whose learning styles were more similar to their field supervisors
   along the active-experimentation-reflective observation continuum would
   rate their field experience higher (Raschick, Maypole, and Day, 1998,
   40). In addition, the authors noted their "own tendencies, as academicians,
   toward excessively abstract and reflective styles," and suggested that they
   "must initially connect with accommodator students' concrete and experimental strengths" (41).
2. Field instructors and students "share a common preference for the accommodator learning style" (Van Soest and Kruzich, 1994, 61). But, "since
   Kolb (1985) asserts that all four stages in the learning cycle are needed
   in order for the most effective learning to occur, it is not assumed that a
   match of field instructor and student based on similar learning styles is
   desirable" (Van Soest and Kruzich, 1994, 61).
3. Social work faculty differed in learning style from both students and field
   instructors by emphasizing abstract conceptualization over concrete experience. That is, faculty were predominantly Convergers, while M.S.W.

students and field instructors were Divergers (Kruzich, Friesen, and Van Soest, 1986).

4. "For both field instructors and students, the greater the difference between them on the concrete experience scale, the more negatively they tended to rate the quality of the relationship and the skills of the other" (Van Soest and Kruzich, 1994, 64). However, the "greater the difference between field instructor and student on the abstract conceptualization scale, the more positively the student tended to rate the field instructor's clinical skills" (Van Soest and Kruzich, 1994, 65). The authors suggest that the former could create learning blocks in the field experience, while the latter suggests learning style differences between field instructor and student need not necessarily result in negative perceptions of the other.

5. There may be sex differences in learning style, with male instructors being Assimilators more significantly than female instructors. Male and female students, however, did not vary significantly in learning styles. These findings on field instructors was reported by Van Soest and Kruzich (1998, 58). Their article did not indicate if women field instructors were accommodators. We'll discuss this further in regard to feminist pedagogy.

6. There may also be age differences in learning styles. Van Soest and Kruzich found "no significant differences between students who are younger and older than the median age for each group" (58). Sims and Sims, however, reported mixed results on the age factor. Some researchers found age not relevant to learning style and, therefore, is not a gauge. One can be a 60–year old with dependent style or an 11–year old with independent style, while others found age important (Sims and Sims, 1995, 197–199).

What, then, may we conclude from the sometimes conflicting findings on teacher-student interaction? First, style compatibility ("fit") may be similar or dissimilar. It would seem that a Converger student would learn more effectively in class with a Converger class teacher than he would with a Diverger field teacher. If, however, the field teacher is a Converger and the student a Diverger, the student may still learn clinical skills effectively because of his respect for that field teacher's clinical analytical skills. This seems to support one of the thinking style principles suggested by Sternberg (1997). That is, styles are socialized by internalization of observed role model attributes.

Second, a style that may fit well in one context (Converger, in class, for instance) may fit less well in another context (the field, which may require more Diverger than Converger style). Third, styles (teacher and student) can change and can be taught. More on this in the discussion on andragogy and pedagogy.

Fourth, that change can occur over the course of time together during the teacher-student interaction. At least two additional articles, though descriptive, provide us with a heuristic bridge between teacher-student interaction and pedagogy-andragogy. Memmot and Brennan (1998, 88) describe the Staged Self-Directed Learning Model (SSDL) developed by Grow (1991). This four-stage model "characterizes students with different degrees of independence (learning style?, M.S.) interaction with faculty providing various types of assistance" (teacher roles, M.S.) (Memmot and Brennan, 1998, 88). Teacher and student roles change as they interact and progress from stage to stage in the learning process. At stage one, the teacher is authority and coach. At stage two, motivation, resource and discussion guide. At stage three, facilitator of discussion and equal participant in the learning groups. At stage four, consultant. In this process, the adult learner student shows decreasing dependence and increasing self direction.

"Just as sequential learning occurs in social work courses, so must it occur in practice" (Tourse, McInnis-Dittrich, and Platt, 1999, 5). According to the authors, the Practice Learning Process (PLP) model "provides students and field instructors with a consistent approach to practice mastery and makes learning and teaching less protracted and more effective" (6). Building on the Diverger form of learning, the authors present a "lateral" sequential model proceeding from simple knowledge and skills to complex knowledge and skills. In short, knowledge progresses "from concrete to abstract through cognitive, affective, and evaluative levels but laterally progresses from simple to complex understanding."

These logically "neat" models, however, do not reflect the complexity of teacher-student interaction in the one (teacher) to more-than-one (students) learning environment with multiple and different learning styles There is no research in this area There are, however, articles, especially by group-work faculty, which provide us with some guidelines. Freeman and Valentine (1998) reviewed the literature on the classroom as a small group which "replicated many of the problems about which the student was studying" (Schwartz, 1964, cited on p.19). Cramer (1995) also reviewed the literature on experiential learning groups as a teaching method, stressing the "mutual aid process in the classroom that parallels the mutual aid process in social work groups" (201). Salmon, Getzel and Kurland use case examples of how the group work teacher can enable the peer group mutual aid process to help: the Neophyte become a "reflective, thinking and feeling worker" (71); the Thinker to learn "that it is all right not to know and to make mistakes" (74); and the Star, before he presents in class, "to be reflective about how he thinks the class will react to his work" (79).

In field teaching, Van Soest and Kruzich also use a case example, although not in a group situation, to demonstrate that "learning styles need to be drawn upon differentially and used flexibly to enhance the field experience" (Van Soest and Kruzich, 1994, 61, 64, 65).

The reflective judgment and critical thinking literature also touch on "shared thought" and the developmental process. Potter and East (2000), review the seven-stage reflective judgment model (RJ) as "an adult cognitive developmental framework for understanding the progression from observation and authority-based ways of knowing, through the acknowledgment of uncertainty to an integrated, personal process for knowing" (223). They stress the importance of 'shared thought" in this process, but emphasize that the group must represent a range of thinking and learning styles which change in composition so that those operating at a slightly higher stage, "draw forward" in development of their reasoning those who operate at a slightly lower stage (learning styles?, M.S) (226, 229).

The EAL (Enquiry and Action Learning) program (Burgess and Jackson, 1990 and cited in Goldstein, 1993. 175) is a prime example of the "shared thought" process designed to educate for reflective thinking. The students "confer with each other, consult with a facilitator, and constantly engage in processes of evaluation" (Goldstein, 1993, 175).

It follows, therefore, that "the teacher's task then becomes to identify each student's learning set (style!, M.S.) as early as possible and by selective individualized responses begin to sort out the complementary transactions that will facilitate the development of an effective learning "environment" (Foeckler and Boynton, 1976, 42).

Andragogy-We come, now, to the third theory (or "approach" or "method" or "model," if you will!) which enables us to complete the framework through which we may interpret the results of our field study. Andragogy changes the balance of power between teacher and student. But "the process of shifting from power and external control by the instructor to empowerment of the learning process by its true constituents takes time" (Romero-Simpson, 1995, 113). The "constituents" (students) are "puzzled by this approach, and not used to it." The academic community (the University) "whose primary concern has traditionally been research and publication" has little interest in that process. Andragogy makes teacher and student co-learners (see Graham, 1997, 33–45). Andragogy makes the teacher a practitioner of science used artistically and creatively.

The social work literature of the past three decades has, from time to time, touched upon these changes. Gelfand, Rohrich, Nevidon and Starak (1975) applied the andragogical model to the training of social workers, finding, among other things, that "the experiential-oriented components (of a course) were more effective than the content-oriented components" (61). Sims (1995, 147–159) also emphasized experiential learning and moving from a pedagogic to an andragogic approach. She states that the "primary role of the teacher, in andragogous teaching is to guide students in their understanding of the student-directed classroom and what responsibilities are entailed in their roles" (153). Relating to the time element and changing teacher roles from early class sessions to mid-class sessions, to later class sessions, Sims shows the movement along the pedagogy-andragogy continuum which helps students "adjust to student-directed learning and set tone or climate that encourages risk-taking and active student participation" (155). Noting that colleges and universities are not committed to this process and do not feel students are mature enough to take charge of their own learning, Sims recommends an incremental approach to change.

Hewitt, the only social work author in the Sims and Sims book (1995, 161–178), presents "facilitator" guidelines for effective adult education, built on Knowles model: Openness, mutual trust, mutual respect, support/challenge/excitement, ability to deal with feelings, and a good sense of humor (partial list!). Sims and Sims (1995, 193–210), provide an operational list of teacher activities such as: combine individual and group assignments, give at least one major oral assignment, show how readings and assignments fit into real-life situations, and provide constant encouragement for students who are slow in understanding or performing or have trouble expressing themselves in writing (partial list, 205–206).

Motivation may be increased by "downplaying grades" while "creating a challenging climate for learning," "promoting cooperative learning" and absenting "competition, threat, or stress from the learning context" (Memmot and Brennan, 1998, 93). High grades, however, "should ideally reflect true learning." "A love of learning should be instilled from the first course session" (Romero-Simpson, 1995, 114). Dalton and Kuhn (1998, 169–184), comparing two teaching methodologies-the lecture discussion model and the cooperative learning model-did indeed find that the latter was more efficacious in terms of long-term knowledge recall and reading significantly more pages of assigned readings. Sternberg, however, questions if it is indeed better for all students than is individual learning (1997, 117), pointing out that "external type" students enjoy working in groups and actively seek them out, whereas "internal type" students "are likely to shy away from groups and prefer to work individually."

A number of factors now begin to fall into place. First, there is a pedagogy-andragogy continuum subject to change over time. Sims, as noted earlier, divides the experiential learning process into early, mid-class and later-class sessions. The first few class sessions, for instance, should include "a concise course description to help students to adjust to student-directed learning and set a tone or climate that encourages risk-taking and active student participation" (1995, 153, 155). During mid-class sessions, the teacher becomes a resource person encouraging students to finalize an ordered topic for each class. In later class sessions, the teacher reviews course accomplishments and student-directed learning, assesses what has been learned (via both oral and written testing), and invites student assessment of worth of self-directed learning for themselves and for their future endeavors.

This developmental process fits well with the SSDL model and the RJ model. In all three, we see the changing role of the teacher (and the students) as they move along the continuum together. Kramer and Wrenn (1994) for instance, present a table of the instructor (teacher) role, adapted from Knowles (1978, 77–79) paralleling conditions of learning, principles of teaching, and implementation techniques. Testing a blend of andragogical and pedagogical teaching methods, they found that "although students found the blending of andragogical and pedagogical teaching methods valuable, many felt there should be even more emphasis placed on pedagogical methods" (60). But the authors stress that "as this study simply describes teaching strategies utilized in two advanced social work practice courses, it is clearly limited in its ability to evaluate the effectiveness of pedagogical and andragogical teaching methods.

Davenport and Davenport, (1988, 83–97) in an article focused on student supervision, refer also to Knowles, review research forming the empirical base of his method, cite the SOQ (Student Orientation Questionnaire) "which operationalizes his theory of andragogy" (83). They, too, relate to teacher (i.e. supervisor) role and technique in the andragogy/pedagogy approaches to individualized student supervision, pointing out that "the educational process would be determined by the logic of the subject matter and content units" (86). Here, they differentiate between pedagogical and andragogical techniques "incorporating these components". The former "would include such transmittal forms as lectures, assigned readings, and canned audiovisual presentations" (86). The latter "would include: group discussion, role playing, skill practice exercises, field projects, action projects, laboratory methods, demonstration seminars, the case method and the critical incident process. Thus, the andragogue is in the role of facilitator, while the pedagogue is the disseminator of information.

Second, in an article on creativity in social work practice, Walz and Uematsu (17–31) stress that the modeling behavior of the instructor can be a foremost instrument". Subtitled (unfortunately and incorrectly, in our opinion): "A pedagogy," they conclude that "teaching creatively comes from an aversion to orthodoxy in content and ritual in practice. It involves a touch of the unexpected (wandering the streets of Florence? M.S.) as well as a high level of student involvement. Creative learning contains elements of discovery and insight. The journey begins without knowing exactly where it will end. The pedagogy (andragogy? M.S.) is planned and mapped, but with an element of destination unknown" (30).

Third, teacher age, like learner age, may not affect orientation on the pedagogy-andragogy continuum. Davenport and Davenport, for instance, note that younger learners need not be "pedagogically-inclined", nor do older learners "automatically become more andragogical" (1988, 84). "Many younger and older students fall into a middle range, apparently preferring a combination of approaches" (84).

Fourth, sex is, however, clearly associated with andragogic orientation. The study of Davenport and Davenport found that female supervisees (learners) "consistently score higher on the andragogical end of the continuum" (91). If we assume that female field instructors are Accomodators (see Van Soest and Kruzich 1994, 58), and we know that social work supervisors and students are accommodators/divergers (see Van Soest and Kruzich, 1994, 61), a picture emerges of a relationship among andragogic orientation, accommodator, and diverger learning style. This means that while classroom teachers tend to exhibit assimilator/converger teaching/learning styles, an andragogic orientation might better suit the concrete experience and feeling needs of their students in the development process between them.

Fifth, we come now to a new nomenclature for class and field teacher. Based on "feminist pedagogy" (we, of course, prefer andragogy!"), the role of instructor is one of midwife, not banker" (Belensky, Clinchy, Goldberger, and Tarule, 1986 cited in Cramer, 1995, 194). The former helps students "articulate and expand their latent knowledge", while the latter "deposits knowledge in the learner's head, the former draws it out" (195). The midwife thus assists the student in "giving birth" to his/her own ideas (sound familiar?). Using this feminist teaching approach, with a class in social group work, the author operationalized "feminist pedagogy" in the classroom via five principles She deemphasized lecture and expert status of the instructor, ulitizing cooperative learning. Course assignments reinforced the concept of students as "instructors and knowers." Students and teacher self disclosure related to course topics "were solicited and supported without the class turning into a therapy group" (where may we ask, were the "red lines?" M.S.). Students had opportunities to assume leadership throughout the course. And learning responsibilities were shared by teacher and students (211). Within this "feminist" framework, the author dealt with a number of issues, two of which are of particular interest to us- grades and expectation fulfillment. She stressed that "grades can be controversial in a feminist classroom" because here egalitarianism seems to end. As for expectations, "classroom dynamics can mirror family life" (Culley, Diamond, Edwards, Lennox, Portuges, 1985, cited in Cramer, 1995, 198). Thus, in addition to being a midwife, the teacher may be viewed as a "mother figure" and may, as well, also have "unconscious feelings and attitudes toward students" (there is our psychoanalytic background, again! M.S.) "Feminist classrooms can be emotional" (198). Does this mean, for instance, that "masculine" classrooms are unemotional? And, incidentally, can the teacher—male or female—be a "father figure."

Basically, this case study raises issues that must be tested more rigorously. How, for instance, does feminist teaching differ from andragogic teaching? Does class composition influence expectation fulfillment (Cramer's class of 18 students included only one male)? Are there, perhaps, "feminist" (accommodator/diverger) learning styles as opposed to "masculine" (assimilator/converger) learning styles? In this study, teaching and learning styles seemed to match!

A second study, based on feminist pedagogy, group process, and classrom evaluation, used a similar midwife approach in nine group work practice courses between 1992–1995. The authors, Freeman and Valentine (1998, 15–29), found that the weekly classroom evaluation questionnaire they developed provided "useful data for improving the course next time it is taught" (25). Although there were no control groups and no statistics were presented, the authors did raise several issues relevant to andragogy in our study. The evaluative process, for instance, promoted a "collegial relationship" between student and instructor. The questionnaire "tracked" group development over time.

"Feeling of safety" increased as the classroom group moved from beginning to middle to end. Although the weekly discussion of evaluation results was time-consuming, the process of student learning was "given depth through application of concepts" (26). Student learning seemed enhanced by the teacher's non-defensiveness in confrontation and "liberal sense of humor."

And now, going back once again, thirty years in time, we discover an additional replacement name for the facilitator role-the dispatcher! In a humorous and deceptively simple article on creative adult learning, Foeckler and Boynton (1976) pulled together many of the concepts described in our monograph. They were indeed precursors of many of the papers cited here. Drawing an analogy to a railway system, they described the learning environment, the student, the teacher, and the significant others "related to or involved in the student's activities as learners" (1976, 37). They viewed the learning environment as the "immovable parts" of the system, the student as train, engineer, and conductor (self-directed learning!), other class members as significant others who may enable or inhibit the student's learning (mutual aid group!), and the dispatcher, whose many responsibilities include charting and encouraging the learning process, communicating information, and interacts openly and honestly as teacher and student learn together on the way to professional competence (facilitator, model, innovator, and risk-taker).

Describing mutual rights and responsibilities, the authors conclude that "the teacher's task then becomes to identify each student's learning set as early as possible and by selective individualized responses begin to sort out the complementary transactions that will facilitate the development of an effective learning environment" (42)

"As if that were not task enough, the teacher also knows that he must balance the needs of a group of adult learners and assist each one in his acquisition of knowledge and skill" (42).

If we de-genderize the "dispatcher" (a male?) and the feminist midwife/mother figure pedagogue (a female?), we may now present a new name of our own-conductor—and a profile of the andragogue. "Conducting" is defined as "the art (or method) of controlling an orchestra . . ., by means of gestures, this control involving the beating of time, ensuring of correct entries, and the 'shaping' of individual phrasing". (Michael Kennedy, 1990, 144). In this analogy, the class is not just a group of pregnant mothers-to-be or a train of students serving as engineers, conductors, and switchmen aided by the dispatcher-teacher, but an orchestra composed of different instruments (learning styles!) The teacher-conductor attempts to unite the individual players in an harmonious group producing the best music (learning!) possible. "There is no explanation beyond the obvious one of psychological personality (charisma?), for the way in which a conductor can, often with a minimum of rehearsal, impose his own style on an orchestra, he may not have encountered before, often completely changing the quality of sound or tone colour even when the orchestra is used to regular performances under another permanent conductor" (144).

Although the "orchestra" (students) can, indeed, "conduct" itself (self-direction!), conductors with or without a baton, can produce beautiful coordination using their "hands only" ("and, of course, their eyes", Kennedy, 1990, 53).

The andragogic teacher, therefore, is mid-wife, parent figure, dispatcher, and conductor all rolled into one, consciously and creatively using her/himself to meet individual and group needs (styles) in a shared developmental learning process.

Chapter Six

Conclusions and Recommendations

Let's see, now, how well we fit this profile in the Andragogic Learning Center in Givat Shmuel. The three following Appendices should help. The first-Andragogic Teaching Check List-summarizes briefly our role performance in the learning process. The Tables in parentheses characterize our activities. Our relationship (Point #12) with the students, for instance, was characterized by breadth, openness and depth. The second Appendix-A New Dictionary for Andragogic Teachers-provides 11 basic concepts which should guide the interventions of any andragogic teacher. We, for instance, relied heavily on group structure in the learning process. The third Appendix-Personal Observations of Study Participants-breathe life into dry statistics, exemplifying vividly the principles of andragogy, the "love" relationship, the educational power of charisma, bridging, the group experience, and time together.

We tried not to "stack" the cards: in our favor, asking only for their impressions of the program. Therefore, we asked the field director, the chairman of the local council and three students who were neither too positive nor too negative during the learning process. They are, as you can see, articulate, but capable of realistic criticism (especially during the many hours we-the teachers-and the group learned together).

All in all, we received professional satisfaction from our findings, their comments and our eight-year labor of love!

What do we recommend for the future?

1. Replication of the Study in American, Canadian, and European Schools of Social Work.
2. More modest hypotheses, such as: "Learning Center students will score at least as well as control group students in certification exam questions."

3. More sensitive measurement instruments. Instead of the TABS question on learning preference, one of the several student learning style inventories already tested for validity and reliability. Instead of a general question about the "ideal" instructor, a ranking of "ideal" instructor characteristics. There should be more group work and community organization questions in the measurement instruments.
4. Class and field teachers, also should complete a Teaching Style Inventory (TSI) or at the very least, the same Learning Style Inventory (LSI) as the students.
5. Teaching-class and field-should be given equal status with research in schools of social work. This means equal pay, equal opportunity for advancement, and equal opportunity for tenure.
6. Doctoral Programs should include a Teaching Track (Specialization).
7. Masters Programs should include a "multi methods" track instead of the traditional casework, community organization, or group work sequence. The latter, incidentally, as noted in the literature, has been sorely neglected as a sequence. As we have shown, group work is an important factor not only in field work (field learning), but also in the learning process itself.
8. A new breed of social worker and teacher (field and class) should be proficient in work with individuals, groups, and communities.
9. There should be more flexibility in classroom time, space, and place (i.e. the learning context). Classroom time, for instance, is now fixed more according to administrative/structural needs rather than according to research findings about time, space and place factors.
10. New faculty members should be chosen on the basis of teaching potential/ability as well as on number and quality of publications.
11. In- service training sessions for young faculty members (class and field) should include principles of andragogy and role and learning theory.
12. A cost analysis comparison should be made between the model presented in this monograph and traditional models of class and field teaching.

Appendix A

Andragogical Teaching Check List

1. Horizontal Learning-Techniques cut across Methods lines
2. Vertical Learning-Methods-specific.
3. Continuum (Teacher Directed-Learner Directed)
   a. Information giving
   b. Information sharing
   c. Information seeking
   Blooming buzzing confusion, but "lurching" forward. Our clear goals for each class session and for the long run were not always clear to learners. This proved frustrating to some (thinkers?) and stimulating to others (feelers, doers). Videotapes of class discussions show this, and some students asked that we should erase the tapes because of the "vehemence" and "turbulence" of the discussions.
4. Use of seven elements of andragogical process design
5. Utilization (artistically) of Kolb's cyclical model (Table 4.1)
6. Our Roles-All seven (Table 4.3)
7. "Good" Teacher/Student Interaction (Table 5.1)
8. Learning Process-All used
9. Knowledge Flow Direction (Two way!)
10. Locus of Control Shift Span of Control (Table 4.2)
11. Expectations and Differentiation among learning styles .
    This consumed "treatment" sector time.
12. Relationship
13. Student participation. Cognitive, Affective, Experiential.

14. Group atmosphere
15. Educational Dilemmas: Generalist, Micro-Mezzo-Macro; Simple to Complex; Class and Field; Bridging.
16. Learning Stages. Includes "shared thought."
17. Facilitator
18. Creativity

A New Dictionary
for Andragogic Teachers

We present here an addition to the role concepts of Biddle, designed to provide a new vocabulary for andragogic teachers.

The 11 concepts culled from the literature should assist the class and field teacher to operationalize the andragogic principles set forth by Knowles and provide a basis for further research.

1. Banking-Knowledge is deposited into the student by the teacher. This concept is rejected by active learning theorists (Rainey and Kolb, 1995, 138) because it views students as passive receptacles for deposits of fixed content from teachers.

2. Currency for Transaction-The opposite of Banking, behavior is the currency for transaction. The amount each (teacher and student) invests (in the learning process) helps to determine the return. This is "the essence of the learning experience!" (Bradford, 1964, 192 cited in Kolb, 1984, 36). "In teaching, for example, I have found it essential to take into account the nature of the subject matter in deciding how to help students learn the material at hand. Trying to develop skills in empathetic listening is a different educational task, requiring a different teaching approach from that of teaching fundamentals of statistics" (Kolb, 1984, 37).

3. Transformation-Learning is the process whereby knowledge is created through the transformation of experience. This definition emphasizes several critical aspects of the learning process as viewed from the experiential perspective.
   a. Emphasis on the process of adaptation and learning as opposed to content or outcome.

b. Knowledge is a transformation process, being continually created and recreated, not an independent entity to be acquired or transmitted. (by the teacher, M.S.)

c. Learning transforms experience in both its objective and subjective forms.

d. To understand learning, we must understand the nature of knowledge and vice versa (Kolb 1984, 38).

4. Contingent Approach-The effectiveness of an instructional method is contingent on both the learning objective to be achieved and the learning style of the participant (Wooldridge, 1995, 64).

5. Learning Maturity-Generally, it would appear that learning maturity is a factor of self-esteem and self-confidence, not chronological factors (Sims and Sims, 1995, 198). An eleven year-old, for instance, can be an independent learner, while a sixty year-old can be a dependent learner.

6. "Onion" Model of Learning-Developed by Curry (cited in Hickcox, 1995), this model consists of three layers. The core, or first layer, presents learning behavior as controlled at a fundamental level by the central personality dimension (of the learner, M.S.). The middle layer centers around a theme of information processing dimension (by the learner, M.S.). The outer layer, the most observable, influenced by the interaction with the environment, is based on the theme of instructional preferences (of the student, M.S.).

7. Single-Loop/Double-Loop Learning-"In general terms, Single-Loop, or first order learning, describes a conservative response to a situation that seeks to maintain the status quo and to uphold existing values and beliefs" (Redmond, 2004, 134, 135). Example: The underlying assumption of a family social worker is that the parents are "hard to work with". Double-Loop, or second-order learning, on the other hand, is "characterized by the search for and exploration of alternative routes, rules, and goals rather than attempting to maintain current routines" (Lant and Mezias, 1999, cited in Redmond, 2004). Example: If the same family social worker realizes that his/her underlying assumption is flawed, and parental anger toward him/her is not viewed as confirmation of the above assumption (hard to work with), then the worker can change the flawed theory, and learn a new frame of reference for working with the parents. (See, also, Argyris, 1991, noted in Murrell and Bishop, 1995, 189,191 from an analogy to a "thinking thermostat").

8. Style-Flex- In some cases, mismatches between the instructor's learning style and the student's learning style can be valuable because this mismatch forces students to stretch or "Style-Flex" as they use their

non-preferred learning modes. By the time students have reached higher education, most are skilled at this adapting. Nevertheless, many still need encouragement in this process (Sims and Sims, 1995, 206).

9. "Pinches"- The non-threatening atmosphere or free-to-learn climate allows each student to bring out in the open her/his "pinches", i.e. feelings of discomfort, concerns, doubts, and frustrations about readings, exercises and other factors in the class (Romero-Simpson, 1995, 111).

10. Critical Conscientiousness-Should be instilled in learners where the meaning of abstract concepts is explored through dialogue among peers. Dialogue is the key to human emancipation of the oppressed (Freire, 1974, cited in Rainey and Kolb, 1995, 138).

11. Group Structures- A variety of group structures should be utilized. Mix groups based on the difference represented in the class-for example, race, gender, learning style, and organization type- and also in a variety of structures of pairs, trios, small groups, and total community. Rainey and Kolb (1995, 144), for instance, found "especially useful" the small group structures they called "learning teams" that met during the formal structure of the class as well as outside the class. Time constraints, class size, and other related factors, they found, did not "allow for the appropriate and thorough processing of student experience within the classroom setting." The teams, however, did allow for continued processing of that experience, and served as support groups for identification of goals and monitoring of progress toward goal achievement. They enrich the learning process, provide a stable reference group, and facilitate trust that spills over into the classroom.

"Armed" with professional knowledge, role theory and these 11 basic concepts, the andragogic teacher (class and field) can, in our estimation, truly influence the learning process. Abandoning the Banking concept for the Currency Transaction concept and building on a Contingency Approach, he/she can transform experience into knowledge.

To do so, he/she must be cognizant of the Learning Maturity of each student, the student's learning layers (Onion model), and Style-Flex. Aiming for Double-Loop Learning and Critical Conscientiousness, the andragogic teacher uses a variety of Group Structures which allow students to express their Pinches on the path to self-directed learning. This is the essence of andragogy, and this, in broader retrospect, is what we did in Givat Shmuel.

Appendix C

Personal Observations of Study Participants

Michal (Class of 1990)—Type 3 Student ("I try to get the most out of classes, and like sharing my ideas with others and getting involved in class activities.")

From a distance of nearly ten years from my participation in the multimethod Project in Givat Shmuel, the positive experience has only become more powerful and clarified—and this I will attempt to detail in the following lines.

Like many students of Social Work, I came to the portals of the University lacking all work experience, completely "green" in theoretical background, and personal and professional maturity.

THE DECISION TO JOIN THE PROJECT

The need to decide which Methods sequence to choose was especially difficult because we had to make our decision by the end of the First year. I was inundated with theoretical knowledge and emotional experiences from the first year of field practice. All this made it difficult for me to decide on the continuation of my learning direction (in the Second year, M.S.). The offer to participate in the encompassing Project, integrating three methods, enchanted me for a number of reasons:

My difficulty in choosing between the Casework and Community Organization Methods. The Project provided an answer which combined both of them.

In light of my unsuccessful and traumatic experience with my First-year Supervisor, I preferred to know beforehand who would be my Second-year Supervisor. I had undergone a crisis of trust which shook my confidence in the professional decisions I made. I felt that in a more controlled project, attached to Academia and teachers, I would be able to strengthen my self-confidence. Purely instinctively, I felt that within the framework of Givat Shmuel, I would be more protected and directed. I hoped that that guidance to a professional life would be greater through a project such as this.

Don't underestimate the following reason! Dr. Sonnheim, I met in my First year, through my mother, who was his student in the past. After one year of studies in the School of Social Work, I understood that frequently, the teacher and his character, his ability to listen, his empathy, his relationship to student and profession, are as important as, if not more so, than the content, the physical place, or the Method he teaches. This is the additional reason I chose the Project.

The group method of learning seemed to me an efficient instrument. Apparently, at that period in my life, I sought intimacy, warm friendship, and I hoped to achieve that indirectly through my academic learning.

Consultation with a friend who just finished participating in the Project with a positive feeling, was certainly a positive influence on my decision.

THE EXPERIENCE

My experience in the Givat Shmuel Project was the highlight of my academic learning. The interesting combination of a dynamic learning group, involvement in the community system, individual professional supervision, and the opportunity to acquire many practice skills, contributed to the formation of my professional self for years to come. In retrospect, after ten years, my decision was a wise one because it was appropriate to my basic personality, and enabled me to give expression to my relative advantages.

The broad rather than narrow involvement, the multidisciplinary work, and the strong group that was built, strengthened my self-confidence and ability. I felt I had the freedom to err, I felt around me a microcosm of the professional world in which I would participate in the future, and that my experiences were a kind of simulation within a protected laboratory. In that laboratory, there was available relevant and genuine group and professional support. My work was valued, but examined in a structured, though caring, sympathetic way.

I participated in the following projects;

1. Two cases—Families in distress
2. A group of children of drug users
3. A community project—Forming a neighborhood committee

All these projects I did with the guidance of Dr. Sonnheim and with the deepening of theoretical knowledge through my participation in the relevant courses.

SUMMARY

For the past six years, I have not worked in the profession, although two years after graduating, I returned to work in Givat Shmuel as Coordinator of Community Drug Abuse Prevention. I filled that post for two and a half years.

ADVANTAGES OF THE LEARNING CENTER FOR ME

As a student, I was exposed to many functions in the community, and this helped me in my future work. My advantage over other candidates stood out because of my acquaintance with the community system.

In all my work after receiving my B.S.W., the skills which I acquired in the Project were evident in:

A systems perspective—Viewing the individual as a part of the social/family/community cosmos, and in light of this, improvement in diagnostic ability of social conditions, use of a repertoire of diagnostic tools for problem treatment (physical place, family genogram, wider connections with the community, and socio-psychological history of the individual).

Organizational survival—I learned and internalized formal ways of working (calling a meeting, "selling" a social idea, drawing up a map of needs, operational definition of need, stages of implementation, its process examination, feedback, etc.), ability to understand organizational structure, political structure, social hierarchy—formal and informal.

Identification of needs, of ability, and positive strengths. In every place, in every organization, ability to discover strengths and abilities is a precondition to create change. Even now, in my position as Director of Human Resources in an organization, this is my first priority.

The belief in change, managing expectations from myself and from my surroundings, in a realistic fashion—this is the key to professional satisfaction and personal happiness. This I learned in the Project. There were failings and disappointments, but also they contributed to learning through the generous help and guiding hand of Dr. Sonnheim.

Yael (Class of 1991)—Student Learning Type 2 ("I prefer highly structured courses and will focus on learning what is required")

It was difficult for me to sit and write about my experience in Givat Shmuel. Eight years after my participation in the Project, I feel that I am now in a different place. The newness, the naivete, and the wish to change are not strange to me, but today I see things with a more realistic and cynical eye.

I chose to participate in the Project because the idea of experiencing three methods—Group Work, Community Organization, and Casework—intrigued me. Also, the youthful and vigorous personality of Dr. Sonnheim succeeded in infecting me with enthusiasm to enter Givat Shmuel and to cause some kind of change. I understood that we would be based within the community itself in order to allow us to absorb the atmosphere of the place in an authentic fashion.

I remember a number of experiences which continue to accompany me during my professional career. One of them was the second-hand clothing shop of Naamat (a Women's volunteer organization, M.S.). It seems to me that we tried to recruit neighborhood women to help in selling and buying clothes. I remember our happiness when we succeeded in enrolling a number of women who, in the past, were in group work treatment. I remember that I led a group of Junior High School children. I remember that as a difficult and castrating experience when the children perceived us as teachers and disparaged us. The second group that I formed consisted of men experiencing certain difficulties. I don't remember the group process, but there was one meeting in which some of the men "opened up" and touched their internal world. This gave me a feeling of contribution and competence.

I remember a sweet young girl suffering from cancer. I treated her primarily through games. Often, I wonder what happened to her. Did she recover?

I remember the supportive and accepting relationship from the social workers And I remember, especially, our walking the length and breadth of Givat Shmuel—visiting homes, community projects, etc. It seems to me this is the proper way to become acquainted with a community—its smells, its voices, its people in the street.

But most importantly, I remember the teamwork among us, the students— the long meetings that continued through the night, during which we raised questions about our work in Givat Shmuel. These meetings were an important part in the formation of my professional life.

It's important to note that this was a heterogeneous group of students. Some were religious, some were non-religious, some were married, but most were single. For me, this was an opportunity to meet different types of girls whom I never would have had a chance to meet intimately, and to share experiences with them.

The atmosphere of cooperation and mutual help, I remember especially. I think that what contributed to that atmosphere was the fact that we had a small house (in the community, M.S.) specifically for collaborative work. This house became a warm "nest" to which the clients came, and from which we ventured out to cooperative activities.

I think that the central purpose of the Project was achieved—our involvement in the life of the community. If previously I perceived Givat Shmuel stigmatically, after my year of studies there, I understood that this was a variegated community composed of a diverse population. I'm certain that we students succeeded in "feeling" the community, in understanding it better, and also our presence was felt by the residents.

I must note that since my participation in the project I have not worked in community organization, but that experience was for me, unique and special. I think that every student should experience community organization before entering the field (of social work, M.S.). The community perspective helped us to view problems at the macro level, and provided us with a broader and more comprehensive outlook.

I remember my supervision as more technical and concrete. It seems to me that there should have been also focus on my feelings and the processes I underwent during my treatment of clients, groups, and community.

I think that the difficulty in this year was primarily our "courting" the target population. Often, it seemed to me that we students "pushed" community projects and groups more than did the community members themselves. This was connected with my own difficulty in using techniques of "courting" them. Because of this, I chose not to work in community organization. Nevertheless, it was important to have this experience in order to understand that this method was not appropriate for me.

In summary, from a distance of eight years, I must say that I experienced a meaningful year, full of experiences and challenges. The combination of three methods (Casework, Group Work, and Community Organization) contributed to my experience as a professional and as a person, and broadened the way I related to my clients,

I think it's important to continue this Project in Field Work and I'm sorry that it was discontinued.

Inbar (Class of 1993)—Student Learning Type 2 ("I prefer highly structured courses and will focus on learning what is required.")

In the following pages, I'll describe my impressions of the Learning Center Project in Givat Shmuel. I participated in this Project in 1993-1994 during my studies for a Bachelor of Social Work degree at Bar Ilan University. This was my second year of studies, and in this project I received professional field supervision (Field Work).

Before I begin to write my impressions, I must comment that I was very moved when Dr. Sonnheim asked me to write a few words to summarize the research that was done. That is because I am very proud today (as I was then) that I was a part of the project, a project which enriched my world as a social worker in particular and my professional world in general, and which in many ways shaped that world.

The purpose of the project was to integrate theoretical learning with field practice. The Learning Center comprised four aspects. The first was professional field practice in the Welfare Services in Givat Shmuel. The second was the formation of a group of students which met once a week with Dr. Sonnheim for theoretical learning but also for discussion of their feelings that arose from their work with clients and their being part of the agency system. The third aspect was individual supervision with almost the same purposes as the group supervision, that included help both as a social worker and as a person (human being). The fourth aspect was theoretical learning of three methods of social work—individual, group, and community.

To begin with, I'll describe the stages of joining the Project. I don't remember the exact content of the presentation of the Project, but the fact that all the students got the impression that this was a serious project with a halo of importance. We were finishing our first year of studies, during which we learned an orientation to the profession, and I was full of motivation to continue my studies in an interesting, educational, and challenging way. The central factor that made the Project prestigious in my eyes, was the selection process. Those who wished to participate in the Project were interviewed, and only after careful screening, candidates were accepted into the Project. An additional factor which was an advantage in the Project was the combination of learning three social work methods. At that point (end of the first year), we were asked to choose between two specializations—Casework-Group Work or Community Organization-Group Work. Learning the three methods resolved my uncertainty about which track to choose. I knew that learning three methods would enrich my professional life in the future.

Those were the reasons I chose to participate in the Project, and I was happy that I was accepted. One of the most meaningful things engraved in my memory was the weekly group meeting. In this meeting, we worked on matters that in "real time" seem important and meaningful, but in retrospect bring a smile to our faces. In this group, we discussed many and varied topics: ranging from the way of passing messages among ourselves, to how the Welfare staff—the clerk, the social workers, and the Director—related to us, and our strong opinions about what is the social work profession. I must note that every topic which seemed important to one of the participants was discussed thoroughly. No topic, whether easy or difficult, was neglected, until a solution was found satisfactory to everyone. For example, my feelings about the assistance or lack thereof by the Department of Community Services in forming a children's group in one of the schools—a project initiated by the Department and run by the students. The problem was raised, presented to all the appropriate parties, and discussed in work group sessions until it was resolved. It's important to note that similar problems were examined by all parties involved—Shlomit Lehman, the Group Work Methods teacher, Dr. Sonnheim, the Project Director and Casework and Community Organization Methods teacher, and, if necessary, additional individuals.

I must emphasize that this year contributed to me in a variety of ways: From the professional aspect alone, learning three methods, as already noted, was important for giving me the opportunity to experience all three. And because of this, later in my work, it was easier for me to approach different projects with a combination of knowledge and experience.

The individual supervision and guidance that I received from Dr. Sonnheim, in its honesty and professional integrity, contributed to my experience, to my self-confidence, and to my success as I continued in the professional world.

My participation in the Project in Givat Shmuel paved my way later as an active participant in a number of areas—the Steering Committee of the Project and a Joint Committee of students and teachers dealing with the Casework Method. When asked to participate in those committees, I responded immediately in the affirmative—something which I ascribe to the supportive, growth-encouraging, creative, and professional atmosphere which I absorbed in the Project.

Reuven Miller, Director of Field Work, School of Social Work, Bar Ilan University

I have been asked to write my impressions of the Teaching and Training Center in Givat Shmuel, which operated between the years 1989-1997. In spite of the years that have elapsed, I remember the Project well. The Proposal, at that time, to establish the Center, was new for Schools of Social Work in Israel and, perhaps, for the world.

Until the Center's establishment in Givat Shmuel, we placed two students with one Supervisor in a Social Service agency, and in some places, four students with two Supervisors. The idea of sending a Unit of twelve students together to one place, with individual and group supervision was new. In addition, the idea that the students would learn in that place also Methods courses was revolutionary.

In the beginning, there were doubts in the School of Social Work if the new idea would succeed. I remember the verbal and written feedback I received from the students at the end of every academic year. I remember the summary meetings that I attended in Givat Shmuel. Both students and staff expressed satisfaction and even enthusiasm over their experiences in Field Work and Methods learning. At the end of each academic year, the student group crystallized in the most positive fashion. The students viewed themselves as a learning community and as change agents.

No student was sent against her/his will to Field Work in Givat Shmuel. The students knew that there would be more hours of study and work than in other placements. Nevertheless, there were many more applications of serious students (for this placement, M.S.) than the Center could absorb.

The Center in Givat Shmuel, during the years, became a "father type" and model for Learning Centers which began to emerge in every possible placement of our School. We were, however, unable to copy exactly the function of the Learning Center in Givat Shmuel. There was no other place that taught Methods courses in the field or taught all three methods. But we were able to introduce the model of eight-twelve students with several supervisors in one placement.

Today (2001), approximately 80% of our students are placed in Learning Centers—in Social Service agencies, Community Mental Health Centers, Hospitals, etc.

You, and the Center in Givat Shmuel were the "pioneers," and your success set for us the direction we are taking now.

Yaacov Vismonski, Former Head of Local Council, Givat Shmuel (1976-1994)

A short time after I was elected Head of the Local Council, I arranged several meetings with the Director General and the President of Bar Ilan University. We decided on close cooperation and much more involvement of the University in the community life of Givat Shmuel.

The idea was that the various Faculties would take advantage of the fact that Givat Shmuel was a relatively small and compact community, appropriate for field work as a laboratory.

The first "pioneer" to implement the decision was the School of Social Work, whose Dean was Professor Reuven Schindler. With great energy, and in cooperation with the Director of Social Services, Givat Shmuel (Haim Cohen), Dr. Moshe Sonnheim and a group of students began to work with older adults, families "at risk," families blessed with many children, and students with learning difficulties. All this, they did primarily in Giora—a neighborhood "in danger."

The central figure in this Project was Dr. Sonnheim who, in my eyes, became almost a citizen of Givat Shmuel. He supervised, helped, and constantly encouraged the students in an exceptional and amazing way to encounter face to face and in practice the clients about whom they learned in theory.

In a short time, the Project became known to all members of our community, broadened and grew in such a way that, through the initiative of Dr. Sonnheim and Mr. Cohen, a place was made available in the community where the students could have a part of their courses (Community Organization, M.S.).

The Givat Shmuel community received very positive reactions and profited greatly from this Project, There is no doubt that in no small measure the success of the Project may be attributed to Dr. Sonnheim who became a much-loved figure in our community.

Bibliography

Aguilar, M.A. (1995). Mexico and Central America. In T.D. Watts, D.Elliot, and N.S. Mayadas (eds.). *International Handbook on Social Work Education*. Westport, Connecticut: Greenwood Press, 61.

Bell, W. (1972). Educational bases for student involvement in the administration of social work schools. In P.J. Stickney (ed.). (1972). *Student Participation in Decision Making in Graduate Schools of Social Work and in Higher Education*. New York: Council on Social Work Education. 41–48.

Berengarten, S. (1957). Identifying learning patterns of individual students: An exploratory study. *Social Service Review*. 31, 407–417

Berengarten, S., and Towle, C. (1964). Notes. Learning Patterns. Prepared for Field Instructors Orientation Session 12/2/64 and not to be used beyond field instructors meeting.

Bernard, L. D. (1995). United States. In T.D. Watts, D. Elliot, and N.S. Mayadas (eds.). (1995). *International Handbook on Social Work Education*. Westport, Connecticut: Greenwood Press, 17–20.

Biddle, B. (1979). *Role Theory: Expectations, Identities, and Behaviors*. New York: Academic Press.

Birnbaum, M.L., and Auerbach, C. (1994). Group work in graduate social work education: The price of neglect. *Journal of Social Work Education*. Fall 1994, Vol. 30 No. 3, 325–335.

Bisno, H., and Cox, F. (1997). Social work education: Catching up with the present and the future. *Journal of Social Work Education*. Vol. 33 No. 2 (Spring/Summer, 1997), 373–387.

Bogo, M., and Globerman, J. (1995). Creating effective university field partnership: An analysis of two interorganizational models for field education. In G. Rogers (ed.) (1995). *Social Work Field Education: Views and Visions*. Dubuque, Iowa: Kendall/Hunt. 17–29.

Bogo, M., Globerman, J. and Sussman, T. (2004). The field instructor as group worker: managing trust and competition in group supervision. *Journal of Social Work Education*. Winter, 2004. V. 40(1), 13–26.

Boud, D. (1985). *Problem-Based Learning in Education for the Professions*. Sydney, Australia: Higher Education Research and Development Authority for Australasia.

Boud, D. and Walker, D. (1990). Making the most of experience. *Studies in Continuing Education*. Vol. 12 No. 2. 61–80.

Boud, D., Keogh, R., and Walker, D. (eds.) (1985). *Reflection: Turning Experience into Learning*. Routledge Palmer. Chapter 1 (18–40).

Bourke, W. (1987). *Social Work Practice Competency Elements*. Faculty of Social Work, University of Toronto, Ontario, Canada.

Burgess, H. (1992). *Problem-Led Learning for Social Work: The Enquiry and Action Approach*. London: Whiting and Birch, Ltd.

Burgess, H., and Jackson, S.(1990). Enquiry and action learning: A new approach to social work education. *Social Work Education*. Vol. 9 No. 3. 3–19.

Caffarella, R.S. (1993). Self-directed learning. In S.B. Merriam (ed.) *An Update on Adult Learning Theory: New Directions for Adult and Continuing Education*. No. 57. Spring, 1993. San Francisco: Jossey-Bass, 25–35.

Candy, P. C. (1991). Self-Direction for Lifelong Learning: A Comprehensive Guide to Theory and Practice. San Francisco: Jossey-Bass.

Candy, P.C. (1991). *Self-Direction for Lifelong Learning A Comprehensive Guide to Theory and Practice*. San Francisco: Jossey-Bass.

Caroff, P. and Matlick, M. (1980). *Social Work in Health Services*. New York: Prodist.

Caspi, J., and Reid, W.J. (2002). *Educational Supervision in Social Work: A Task-Centered Model for Field Instruction and Staff Development*. New York: Columbia University Press.

Cavaliere, I.A. (1992). The Wright brothers' odyssey: Their flight of learning. In A. Cavaliere and A. Sgroi. (eds.). *Learning for Personal Development: New Directions for Adult and Continuing Education*. No. 53. San Francisco: Jossey Bass.

Chen, D. (1995). *Education Toward the Twenty-First Century*. Tel Aviv, Israel. Ramot. 20th Anniversary Publication of the School of Education, Tel Aviv University. (Hebrew).

Cloward, R. (1998). Letter in *Social Work*. NASW, Washington, D.C.: November, 1998. Vol. 43, No.6, 584–586.

Coleman, H., Collins, D., and Aikins, D. (1995). The student-at-risk in the practicum. In G. Rogers (ed.). (1995). *Social Work Field Education: Views and Visions*. Dubuque, Iowa: Kendall/Hunt, 256–267.

Council on Social Work Education (1994). Handbook of Accreditation Standards and Procedures. CSWE.

Council on Social Work Education. (1994). Education Curriculum Policy Statement for Master's Degree Programs. (1994).

Cox, D. (1995). Asia and the Pacific. In T.D. Watts, D. Elliot, and N.S. Mayadas (eds.). (1995). *International Handbook on Social Work Education*. Westport, Connecticut: Greenwood Press, 321–338.

Cramer, E.P. (1995). Feminist pedagogy and teaching social work practice with groups: A case study. *Journal of Teaching in Social Work.* Vol, 11 No. 1. (1995), 193–215.

Dalton, B., and Kuhn, A.C. (1998). Researching teaching methodologies in the classroom. *Journal of Teaching in Social Work.* Vol. 17 No 1/2. (1998), 169–184.

Davenport, J.A., and Davenport, J. III.(1988). Individualizing student supervision: The use of andragogical-pedagogical orientation questionnaires. *Journal of Teaching in Social Work.* Vol. 2 No. 2 (1988), 83–97.

Elad, N. with Arkin, N., Ben-Meir, S., Gur, R., Gilad, D., and Weiner, A. (1989). *Learning Centers: Structures Connecting Academic and Field: Accomplishments and Dilemmas.* University of Haifa, School of Social Work. Haifa, Israel: (Hebrew).

Feldman, R. (1972). Towards the evaluation of teaching competence in social work. *Journal of Education for Social Work.* Vol. 8, No. 2, (Spring 1972). 5–15.

Feyrer, J., and Whitaker, W. (1995). Student empowerment: Models for the practicum placement process. In Rogers, G. (ed.) (1995). *Social Work Field Education: Views and Visions.* Dubuque, Iowa: Kendall/Hunt, 341–350.

Foeckler, M.M., and Boynton, G. (1976). Creative adult learning—teaching: Who's the engineer of this train? *Journal of Education for Social Work.* Fall, 1976, Vol. 12, No.3, 37–43.

Freeman, I., and Hansen, F.C. (1995). Field instructors' perceptions of the social work education process. In G. Rogers (ed.) (1995). *Social Work Field Education: Views and Visions.* Dubuque, Iowa: Kendall/Hunt, 294–312.

Freeman, M.L., and Valentine.D. (1998). The connected classroom: Modeling the evaluation of practice by evaluating the classroom group. *Journal of Teaching in Social Work.* Vol. 17 No. 1/2 (1998), 15–29.

Gambrill, E. (1995). The role of critical thinking in social work. Class of 1954 Lecture in honor of Dr. Anita Faatz, University of Pennsylvania, School of Social Work, February 2, 1995. Mimeographed.

Gardiner, D. (1989). *The Anatomy of Supervision.* Philadelphia: Open University Press.

Gelfand, B., Rohrich, S., Nevidon, P., and Starak, I. (1975). An andragogical application to the training of social workers. *Journal of Education for Social Work.* 11(3), 55–61.

Gibbs, P., and Blakely, E.H. (2000). *Gatekeeping in B.S.W. Programs.* New York: Columbia University Press.

Glassman, U. (1995). Introduction to field instructor roles and processes. In D. Schneck, B. Grossman, and U. Grossman (eds.). *Field Education in Social Work: Contemporary Issues and Trends.* Dubuque, Iowa: Kendall/Hunt. 185–192.

Goldberg-Wood, G, and Middleman, R.R. (1991). Principals that guide teaching. *Journal of Teaching in Social Work.* V. 5. No. 2. 111–116.

Goldstein, H. (1984). *Social Learning and Change: A Cognitive Approach to Human Services.* New York and London: Tavistock Publications.

Goldstein, H. (1993). Field education for reflective practice: A re-constructive proposal. *Journal of Teaching in Social Work.* Vol. 8, No. 1/2, 165–182; and in

J. Laird (ed.). *Revisioning Social Work Education: A Social Constructionist Approach*. 1993, 165–182.

Goldstein, H. (2001). *Experiential Learning: A Foundation for Social Work Education and Practice*. Alexandria, Virginia: Council on Social Work Education.

Gould, N., and Taylor, I. (eds.) (1996). *Reflective Learning for Social Work: Theory and Practice*. Aldershot, Hants, England: Arena.

Graham, M.A. (1997). Empowering social work faculty: Alternative paradigms for teaching and learning. *Journal of Teaching in Social Work*. Vol. 15 No. 1/2 (1997), 33–45.

Gross, G.M. (1981). Cited in M. Urbanowski, and M. Dwyer (1988). Learning Through Field Instruction: A Guide for Teachers and Students. Milwaukee, Wisconsin: Family Service Association of America, 63.

Grossman, B., Levine-Jordano, N., and Shearer, P. (1991). Working with students' emotional reactions in the field: An education framework. In D. Schneck, B. Grossman, and U. Glassman (eds.). (1991). *Field Education in Social Work: Contemporary Issues and Trends*. Dubuque, Iowa: Kendall/Hunt Publishing Company, 205–216.

Guttman, D., and Cohen, B.Z. (1995). Israel. In T.D. Watts, D. Elliot, and N.S. Mayadas (eds.). (1995). *International Handbook on Social Work Education*. Westport, Connecticut: Greenwood Press, 314.

Hamilton, N., and Else, J.F. (1983). *Designing Field Education: Philosophy, Structure, and Process: Philosophy, Structure, and Process*. Springfield, Illinois: Charles E. Thomas

Hampson, S.J. (1995). Zimbabwe. In T.D. Watts, D. Elliot, and N.S. Mayadas (eds.). (1995). *International Handbook on Social Work Education*. Westport, Connecticut: Greenwood Press, 255.

Harris, A. (1996). Learning from experience and reflection in social work education. In N. Gould and I. Taylor (eds.) (1996). Reflective Learning for Social Work. Aldershot: Arena, 42.

Hartman, C., and Willis, R.M. (1991). The gatekeeper role in social work: A survey. In D. Schneck, B. Grossman, and U. Glassman (eds.) (1991). Field Education in Social Work: Contemporary Issues and Trends. Dubuque, Iowa: Kendall/Hunt, 310–319.

Hativa, N., and Raviv, A. (1995). University instruction, evaluation, and alternative models to improve it. In D. Chen (ed.). *Education Toward the Twenty-First Century*. Tel Aviv: Ramot. 20th Anniversary Publication of the School of Education, Tel Aviv University, (Hebrew), 447–459.

Hawthorne, L., and Holtzman, R.F. (1991). The open expression of differences in the field practicum: Report of a pilot study. In D. Schneck, B. Grossman, and U. Glassman (eds.). (1991). *Field Education in Social Work: Contemporary Issues and Trends*. Dubuque, Iowa: Kendall/ Hunt Publishing Company, 320–328.

Hewitt, R.L. (1995). The nature of adult learning and effective training guidelines. In R.R. Sims, and S.J. Sims (eds.). (1995). *The Importance of Learning Styles*. Westport, Connecticut: Greenwood, 161–178.

Hickcox, L.H. (1995). Learning styles: A survey of adult learning style inventory models. In R.R. Sims, and S.J. Sims (eds.). (1995). *The Importance of Learning Styles*. Westport, Connecticut: Greenwood, 25–47.

Hokenstad, M.C., and Rigby, B.D. (1977). *Participation in Teaching and Learning: An Idea Book for Social Work Education*. New York: International Association of Schools of Social Work.

Hunt, D.E. (1971). Cited in M. Urbanowski, and M. Dwyer (1988). Learning Through Field Instruction: A Guide for Teachers and Students. Milwaukee, Wisconsin: Family Service Association of America, 63.

Johnston, N., Rooney, R., and Reitmeir, M. A. (1991). Sharing power: Student feedback to field supervisors. In D. Schneck, B. Grossman, and U. Glassman (eds.). (1991). *Field Education in Social Work: Contemporary Issues and Trends*. Dubuque, Iowa: Kendall/Hunt Publishing Company, 198–204.

Kennedy, M. (1990). Conducting; Baton. *The Concise Oxford Dictionary of Music*. Oxford: Oxford University Press, 53,144.

Kilpatrick, A.C., Thompson, K.H., Jarrett, H.H., Jr., and Anderson, R.J. (1984). Social work education at the University of Georgia. In M.S. Knowles and Associates (eds.). *Andragogy in Action: Applying Modern Principles of Adult Learning*. *London and San Francisco: Jossey-Bass, 243–263*.

Kindelsperger, W. L. (1968). (ed.) Modes of formal adult learning in preparation for the service professions. Council on Social Work Education. *Field Learning and Teaching: Exploration in Graduate Social Work Education*. New York: Council on Social Work Education

Knight, C. (1996). A study of MSW and BSW students' perceptions of their field instructors. *Journal of Social Work Education*, Vol. 32, No.3 (Fall 1996), 399–414.

Knight, C. (2001). The process of field instruction: BSW and MSW students' views of effective field supervision. *Journal of Social Work Education*. Vol. 37, No. 2 (Spring/Summer, 2001), 357–379.

Knight, C. (2001). The skills of teaching social work practice in the generalist/foundation curriculum: BSW and MSW student views. *Journal of Social Work Education*. Vol. 37, No. 3. (Fall 2001) 507–521.

Knowles, M.S. (1972). Innovations in teaching styles and approaches based upon adult learning. *Journal of Education for Social Work*. 8(2). 32–39. Spring, 1972.

Knowles, M.S. (1975). *Self-Directed Learning*. New York: Association Press.

Knowles, M.S. (1980). *The Modern Practice of Adult Learning*. (Revised ed.). Chicago: Association Press/Follett.

Knowles, M.S. (1984). *Andragogy in Action: Applying Modern Principles of Adult Learning*. London and San Francisco: Jossey-Bass.

Kolb, D.A. (1984). *Experiential Learning*. Englewood Cliffs, New Jersey: Prentice-Hall.

Kramer, B.J., and Wrenn, R. (1994). The blending of andragogical and pedagogical teaching methods in advanced social work practice courses. *Journal of Teaching in Social Work*. Vol. 10. No. 1/2 (1994).

Kruzich, J., Friesen, B., and Van Soest, D. (1986). Assessment of student and faculty learning styles: Research and application. *Journal of Social Work Educaiton.* 22(3), 22–30.

Kurland, R. (1991). The classroom teacher and the role of authority. *Journal of Teaching in Social Work.* Vol. 5(2), 81–94.

Lager, P.B., and Robbins, V.C. (2004). *Journal of Social Work Education.* Vol. 40 No.1 (Winter, 2004). Guest Editorial. Special Section: Field education in social work, 1–11.

Lager, P.B., and Robbins, V.C., Co-Chairs on Social Work Education Commission on Field Education (2004). Field Education: Exploring the future, expanding the vision. *Journal of Social Work Education.* Winter 2004, Vol. 40 No.1, 3–11.

Lemberger, J., and Marshack, E.F. (1991). Educational assessment in the field: An opportunity for teacher learner mutuality. In D. Schneck, B. Grossman, and U. Glassman (eds.). (1991). *Field Education in Social Work: Contemporary Issues and Trends.* Dubuque, Iowa: Kendall/Hunt Publishing Company, 187–197.

Lennon, T.M. (2004). *Statistics on Social Work Education in the United States: 2002.* Alexandria, Virginia: Council on Social Work Education.

Lewis, H. (1991). Teacher's style and use of professional self in social work education. *Journal of Teaching in Social Work.* Vol. 5(2), 1991, 24, 27.

Loewenberg, F. M. (1978). Core themes in social work education. Revised version of paper presented to XIXth International Congress of Schools of Social Work, August 15, 1978, Jerusalem, Israel. Mimeographed.

Lowy, L. (1968). Wither social work education amid social change? *Journal of Education for Social Work.* Vol. 4. No. 1 (Spring, 1968). 31–36.

Lowy, L. (1978). Teaching and learning in social work education---what do studies tell us? Paper presented to XIXth International Congress of Schools of Social Work, August 15th, 1978. Jerusalem, Israel. Mimeographed.

Lowy, L.M., Bloksberg, H.J., and Walberg, H.J. (1971) *Integrative Learning and Teaching in Schools of Social Work.* New York: Association Press, 1971.

Mandal, K.S. (1995). India. In T.D. Watts, D. Elliot, and N.S. Mayadas (eds.). (1995). *International Handbook on Social Work Education.* Westport, Connecticut: Greenwood Press, 362–364.

Marschack, E.F. (1991). The older student: Social work's new majority. In D. Schneck, B. Grossman, and U. Glassman (eds.). (1991). *Field Education in Social Work: Contemporary Issues and Trends.* Dubuque, Iowa: Kendall/Hunt Publishing Company, 295–300.

McMurty, S.L., and McClelland, R.W. (1997). Trends in student-faculty ratios and the use of non-tenure track faculty in MSW programs. *Journal of Social Work Education.* Vol. 33 No. 2 (Spring/Summer 1997). 293–306.

McMurty, S.L., and McClelland, R.W. (1997). Class sizes, faculty workloads, and program structures: How MSW programs have responded to changes in their environment. *Journal of Social Work Education.* V. 33, No. 2 (Spring/Summer, 1997), 307–320.

Memmot, J., and Brennan, E.M. (1998) Learner-learning environment fit: An adult learning model for social work education. *Journal of Teaching in Social Work.* Vol. 16(1/2), 1998.

Meron, M. (1995). Who is "the good student?" In D. Chen (ed.) *Education Toward the Twenty-First Century.* Tel Aviv: Ramot. 20th Anniversary Publication of the School of Education, Tel Aviv University. (Hebrew). 439–446.

Merriam, S.B. (1993). *An Update on Adult Learning Theory: New Directions for Adult and Continuing Education.* No. 57. Spring, 1993. San Francisco: Jossey-Bass

Merriam, S.B. (1993). Adult learning: Where have we come from? Where are we headed? In S.B. Merriam (ed.). *An Update on Adult Learning Theory: New Directions for Adult Continuing Education.* No. 57, Spring, 1993, 5–14

Middleman, R. (1987). (2nd Ed.). *A Study Guide for ACSW Certification.* Silver Spring, MD.: NASW.

Miller, J., Kovacs, P., Wright, L., Corcoran, J., and Rosenblum, A. (2005). Field education: Student and field instructor perceptions of the learning process. *Journal of Social Work Education.* V. 41, No. 1 (Winter, 2005), 131–145.

Montgomery County School Alliance. (1971). A student voice. In R. and B. Gross (eds.). *Radical School Reform.* London: Victor Gollancz, Ltd. 147–160.

Murrell, K.L., and Bishop, R.W. (1995). The learning model for managers: A tool to facilitate learning. In R.R. Sims, and S.J. Sims (eds) (1995). *The Importance of Learning Styles.* Westport, Connecticut: Greenwood, 189–191.

Navari, S. (1991). The implications of part-time programs for field work models: Provocative dilemmas and conceptual frameworks. In D. Schneck, B. Grossman, and U. Glassman. (eds.). (1991). *Field Education in Social Work: Contemporary Issues and Trends.* Dubuque, Iowa: Kendall/Hunt Publishing Co., 272–287.

Neufeld, V.R. and Barrows, H.S. (1984) Preparing medical students for life-long learning. In M.S. Knowles (ed.). *Andragogy in Higher Education.* 207–226.

Ntusi, T. (1995). South Africa. In T.D. Watts, D. Elliot, and N.S. Mayadas (eds.). (1995). *International Handbook on Social Work Education.* Westport, Connecticut: Greenwood Press, 274.

O'Neal, G.S. (1996). Enhancing undergraduate student participation through active learning. *Journal of Teaching in Social Work.* Vol. 13 No.1 1996, 141–155.

Potter, C.C., and East, J.F. (2000). Developing reflective judgment through MSW education. *Journal of Teaching in Social Work.* Vol. 20 No. 1/2 2000, 217–237.

Pratt, D.D. (1988). Andragogy as a relational construct. *Adult Education Quarterly.* 1988, No 38. 160–181.

Pratt, D.D. (1993). Andragogy after twenty-five years. In S.B. Merriam (ed.). (1993). *An Update on Adult Learning theory. New Directions for Adult and Continuing Education.* No. 57, Spring, 1993. San Francisco: Jossey-Bass, 15–23

Ragab, I.A. (1995). Middle East and Egypt. In T.D. Watts, D. Elliot, and N.S. Mayadas (eds.). (1995). *International Handbook on Social Work Education.* Westport, Connecticut: Greenwood Press, 297.

Rainey, M.A. and Kolb, D.A. (1995). Using experiential learning theory and learning styles in diversity education. In R.R. Sims and S.J. Sims (eds.). (1995). *The Importance of Learning Styles.* Westport, Connecticut: Greenwood, 136,138.

Raphael, F.B., and Rosenblum, A.F. In D. Schneck, B. Grossman, and U. Glassman (eds.). (1991). *Field Education in Social Work: Contemporary Issues and Trends.* Dubuque, Iowa: Kendall/ Hunt Publishing Company, 301–309.

Raschick, M., Maypole, D.E., and Day, P.A. (1998). Improving field education through Kolb learning theory. *Journal of Social Work Education.* Vol. 34, No.1 (Winter 1998). 31–42.

Redmond, B. (2004). Reflecting on practice: Exploring individual and organizational learning through a reflective teaching model. In N. Gould, and M. Baldwin (eds.). (2004). *Social Work, Critical Thinking and the Learning Organization.* Aldershot, England: Ashgate, 129–142.

Rogers, G. (1996). Training field instructors British style. *Journal of Social Work Education.* Vol. 32. No. 2 (Spring/Summer 1996). 265–276.

Romero-Simpson, J.E. (1995). The importance of learning styles in total quality management-oriented college and university courses. In R.R. Sims, and S.J. Sims (eds.) (1995). *The Importance of Learning Styles.* Westport, Connecticut: Greenwood, 99–115.

Rothman, B. (1973). Perspectives on learning and teaching. *Journal of Education for Social Work.* Vol. 9, No. 2, 1973, 39–52.

Salmon, R., Getzel, G., and Kurland, R. (1991). The neophyte, the natural, the thinker, and the star. *Journal of Teaching in Social Work.* V. 5(1), 1991, 65–80.

Schneck, D. (1995). The promise of field education in social work. In G. Rogers (ed.). (1995). *Field Education: Views and Visions.* Dubuque, Iowa: Kendall/Hunt.

Schon, D.A. (1983). *The Reflective Practitioner: How Professionals Think in Action.* New York: Basic Books.

Schubert, M.S. (1969). An overview of field instruction: making the best use of traditional and atypical field placements. In B.L. Jones. (ed.) *Current Patterns in Field Instruction in Graduate Social Work Education.* New York: Council on Social Work Education.

Seelig, J.M. (1991). Social work and the critical thinking movement. *Journal of Teaching in Social Work.* Vol. 5 No. 1 (1991), 21–33.

Shulman, L. (1987). The hidden group in the classroom: The use of the group process in teaching group work practice. *Journal of Teaching in Social Work.* Vol. 1 No. 2. 3–31.

Sims, R.R., and Sims, S.J. (1995). Learning and learning styles. In R.R. Sims and S.J. Sims (eds.). (1995). *The Importance of Learning Styles.* Westport, Connecticut. Greenwood, 198.

Sims, R.R., and Sims, S.J. (eds.). (1995). *The Importance of Learning Styles.* Westport, Connecticut: Greenwood.

Sims, S.J. (1995). Experiential learning: Preparing students to move from the classroom to the work environment. In R.R. Sims and S.J. Sims (eds.). (1995). *The Importance of Learning Styles.* Westport, Connecticut: Greenwood, 147–159.

Sonnheim, M. (1968). *Role Deprivation in Social Caseworkers: A Professional Dilemma.* Unpublished Doctoral Thesis. (1968). School of Applied Social Sciences, Case Western Reserve University, 3–5.

Sonnheim, M. (1988). *Techniques of Social Intervention with Groups* (Hebrew). Jerusalem, Israel: Academon.

Sonnheim, M. (1993). Techniques of intervention with groups. *Journal of Social Work and Policy in Israel: Theory, Research, and Practice.* Vols. 7–8., 125–144. Jerusalem, Israel: Bar Ilan University Press.

Sowers-Hoag, K., and Thyer, B. (1985). Teaching social work practice: A review and analysis of empirical research. *Journal of Social Work Education.* 21(3), Fall, 1985, 5–15.

Sternberg, R.J. (1997). *Thinking Styles.* Cambridge, U.K.: Cambridge University Press.

Swanson, E.A. (1972). Student involvement in the governance of schools of social work: Implications for social work education and practice. In P.J. Stickney (ed.). (1972). *Student Participation in Decision Making in Graduate Schools of Social Work and in Higher Education.* New York: Council on Social Work Education, 77–83.

Szewello, A. H., and Shragge, E. (1995). Community-based field placements: Recent innovations. In G. Rogers (ed.) (1995). *Social Work Field Education: Views and Visions.* Dubuque, Iowa: Kendall/Hunt, 92–105.

TABS (Teaching Analysis by Students). Clinic to Improve University Teaching. School of Education, University of Massachusetts at Amherst. (Undated). Question No. 47.

Thelen, H. (1967). Group interactional factors in learning. In E.M. Bower and W.G. Hollister (eds.). *Behavioral Science Frontiers in Education.* New York: John Wiley and Sons, 257.

Thomlinson, B., and Collins, D. (1995). Use of structured consultation for learning issues in field education. In G. Rogers (ed.) *Social Work Field Education: Views and Visions.* Dubuque, Iowa: Kendall/Hunt. 223–228.

Tough, A. (1979). *The Adult's Learning Projects: A Fresh Approach to Theory and Practice in Adult Learning.* (2nd Ed.). Toronto: Ontario Institute for Studies in Education.

Tourse, R.W.C., McInnis-Dittrich, and Platt, S. (1999). The road to autonomous practice: A practice competency teaching approach for supervision. *Journal of Teaching in Social Work.* Vol. 19 No. 1/2 1999.

Towle, C. (1963). The place of help in supervision. Paper presented at Simmons College School of Social Work. Mimeographed.

University of Pennsylvania (1990). *The Penn Approach: An Evolving Philosophy of Education for Social Work Practice.* Philadelphia, Pennsylvania: 1–20.

Urbanowski, M., and Dwyer, M. (1988). *Learning Through Field Instruction: A Guide for Teachers and Students.* Milwaukee, Wisconsin: Family Service of America Press.

Valentine, D.P., Edwards, S., Gohagan, D., Huff, M., Pereira, A., and Wilson, P. (1998). Preparing doctoral students for teaching: Report of a survey. *Journal of Social Work Education.* Vol. 34 No. 2, (Spring/Summer, 1998), 273–281.

Van Soest, D., and Kruzich, J. (1994). The influence of learning styles on student and field instructor perceptions of field placement success. *Journal of Teaching in Social Work.* Vol. 9 No. 1/2 (1994), 49–69.

Walker, W. L. (1972). Changing thought and action styles of students and faculty: Imperatives for social work education. *Journal of Social Work Education.* Vol. 8, No. 1. (Winter, 1972). 56–63.

Walz, T., and Uematsu, M. (1997). Creativity in social work practice: A pedagogy. *Journal of Teaching in Social Work.* Vol. 15 No. 1/2 (1997), 17–31.

Watts, T.D. Introduction. In T.D. Watts, D. Elliot, and N.S. Mayadas (eds.). (1995). *International Handbook on Social Work Education.* Westport, Connecticut: Greenwood Press, 3.

Wilson, A.L. (1993). The promise of situated cognition. In S.B. Merriam (ed.).(1993). *An Update on Adult Learning Theory. New Directions for Adult and Continuing Education.* No. 57. Spring, 1993, 71–79.

Wilson, S. (1981). *Field Instruction: Techniques for Supervision.* New York: The Free Press. 89.

Wodarski, J. (1986). *An Introduction to Social Work Education.* Springfield, Illinois:Charles Thomas.

Wooldridge, B. (1995). Increasing the effectiveness of University/College instruction: Integrating the results of learning style research into course design and delivery. In R.R. Sims and S.J. Sims (eds.). (1995). *The Importance of Learning Styles.* Westport, Connecticut: Greenwood, 49–67.

Wrightsman, L.S. (1994). *Adult Personality Development: Theories and Concepts.* Thousand Oaks: Sage.

Breinigsville, PA USA
14 December 2009
229169BV00003B/3/P